Narrative Situations in the Novel

**TOM JONES, MOBY-DICK,
THE AMBASSADORS, ULYSSES**

FRANZ STANZEL

Narrative Situations in the Novel

TOM JONES, MOBY-DICK,

THE AMBASSADORS, ULYSSES

Translated by James P. Pusack

INDIANA UNIVERSITY PRESS

Bloomington / London

Originally published as Die
typischen Erzählsituationen im Roman by
Wilhelm Braumüller, Universität-Verlagsbuchhandlung
G. m. b. H., Vienna.

Copyright © 1971 by Indiana University Press

Published in Canada by Fitzhenry & Whiteside Limited, Don Mills, Ontario

Library of Congress catalog card number: 70-138411

ISBN: 253-33970-7

Manufactured in the United States of America

CONTENTS

91304

Narrative Situations in the Novel

**TOM JONES, MOBY-DICK,
THE AMBASSADORS, ULYSSES**

INTRODUCTION

Each year the American book trade publishes almost two thousand novels. Similar data obtain for England and Germany.[1] Yet it seems precipitate to call the present the age of the novel. When one observes how, in this flood of semiliterary and subliterary works, the novel stands in constant danger of losing its own peculiar contours, one is inclined to speak rather of a crisis of the novel in the present. To be sure, as a currently fashionable genre the novel attracts numerous authors, but only a few of these authors make demands of its capabilities as a form for the literary creation of reality. Many authors never discover the crucial differences in design and intention between the truly literary presentation of the world and the everyday type attempted in countless newspaper stories, police documents, case histories, sociological reports, and the like. Often such an author is moved by authentic feelings which may arise from honest indignation or from a deeply felt belief or ideology. Rather than give these feelings adequate formal expression and effectiveness in an essay, a manifesto, or a polemic, he forces them into a novelistic guise. This guise may very well serve his purposes by bringing the message to a broad reading public, but it is frequently quite inadequate as a literary creation. Occasionally, of course, a truly artistic creation may ensue. This cannot be denied. The demanding reader, however, will still feel a definite lack of satisfaction at the end of such novels. Virginia Woolf describes this reaction in a polemic against the works of the "Edwardians," Wells, Galsworthy, and Bennett:

> Sometimes I wonder if we are right to call them books at all. For they leave one with so strange a feeling of incompleteness and dissatisfaction. In order to complete them it seems necessary to do something—to join a society, or, more desperately, to write a cheque. That done, the restlessness is laid, the book finished; it can be put upon the shelf, and need never be read again.
>
> *(The Captain's Death Bed, p. 99)*

Virginia Woolf does the novels of these authors an injustice, but she does point up an aspect of a true work of art which these three authors found more or less unimportant. It is an aspect which this study will treat with particular attention. Since the fundamental premise of this investigation is that every work of art, but particularly the literary work, offers as many aspects for interpretation as there are methods available, it is not necessary to justify the approach taken here. The novel is seen here exclusively as a literary work of art, the reading of which requires no other motivation than the expectation of the pleasure the work promises the reader. From this point of view the preponderance of ulterior motives in a novel seems to be at variance with authentic literary purpose. Authentic literary purpose can only be attained through time spent in static lingering with the work; in "quiet contemplation of the metaphysical qualities," such as the tragic, the sinful, the grotesque, the fascinating.[2] If this goal of the novel is not reached in the majority of creative attempts, then the novel form must gradually fall prey to a utilitarian banalization which will conceal its true capabilities. A number of voices have already called attention to this critical turn of events.[3] It would be a worthwhile task for literary historians to investigate more fully the motives which bring certain authors to prefer the novel form to some other form which in many cases may be more appropriate—the essay, the biography, the autobiography, the feuilleton, or the psychoanalytic case history.

In view of these circumstances the state of affairs in the realm of literary theory is of particular importance. While the lyric and dramatic genres can lay claim to a secure body of theory, the novel still finds itself in a rather precarious position. The reasons for this lie above all in the fact that the novel—in comparison to other literary genres and forms—has traditionally been held in very low esteem.[4] Schiller has quite high praise for such individual authors as Cervantes, Fielding, and Wieland, but the novelist is for him only the poet's "half-brother."[5] The reading public has always considered the novel a more readily accessible and therefore inferior literary form: "And what are you reading, Miss—?" "Oh, it is only a novel" (*Northanger Abbey*, Chapter 5). Jane Austen is renowned as one of the first to combat this view with irony and parody. It is quite symptomatic of the state of novel theory that such an established critic as Emil Staiger can attempt to define the "genre ideas" of the lyrical, the epical, and the dramatical without devoting the least attention to the novel. Staiger bases his definition of the epical mode exclusively on verse epics, particularly on those of Homer.[6] Such approaches to genre poetics are naturally not likely to rid the novel of its demirespectability. Nor can such definitions of the novel be of much help in differentiating the generic qualities of the novel from those of the drama or lyric poetry. The fact that the novel belongs to the epic genre has been sufficiently documented by Rafael Koskimies; this question needs no further examination here.[7] Because of this proximity of epic and novel, theorists of the novel have often taken the less amorphous forms of the epic as their starting point. Yet despite the numerous, very fruitful results of this approach the theory of the novel appears nevertheless to have been slighted. Even the quasi-normative importance frequently attributed to the visible presence of a personal narrator can be shown on closer examination to be a generalization of a characteristically epic narrative principle. This principle, however, only holds true for a specific form of the novel. Discussion of the relevant theories of Käte Friedemann, Robert Petsch, Julius Petersen, and Wolfgang Kayser will be taken up when the context necessitates referring to their views.

The present investigation takes as its point of departure one central feature of the novel—its mediacy of presentation. Mediacy or indirectness also characterizes the technique of presentation in the epic. In this sense, then, the epic and the novel represent members of the same fundamental literary genre. The difference between the two lies in the spectrum of narrative guises each can employ. For these theoreticians the novel's mediacy of presentation consists of the presence of a personal narrator. Here, however, the concept of mediacy will also be viewed from the perspective of the reader. This study will show that there is one type of novel in which the presence of a personal narrator does not attain any kind of tangible reality in the reader's imagination. The view that authentic presentation in the novel is only possible through the mediation of a personal narrator is as untenable a normative criterion as the view, held notably by Friedrich Spielhagen,[8] that the narrator ought to remain fully invisible. Keeping this limitation in mind it is possible to make use of the concept of the mediacy of presentation developed in several earlier studies. The concept of mediacy, for example, was noted by Robert Petsch.[9] Käte Friedemann even holds that in the reader's imagination the mediative process takes ontic precedence over the narrated events.[10] Common to all these views is the belief that it is primarily the figure of the narrator in one of his many possible guises which is concretized by the reader. The narrator then mediates the potential fictional world. In him the reader's mental illusion finds the bridge and the road which lead into the land of fiction. The basic situation of the mediative process, however, is capable of a number of variations. As a rule the narration in a given novel maintains a single fixed type of mediative process throughout the work. This mediative process will be called the *narrative situation*. The mediacy of the novel finds its concrete expression in the narrative situation: one author narrates the facts he has learned about a given subject; another appears as the editor of a manuscript; yet another writes letters or narrates his own experiences.

These are only a few common guises of the narrative situation. Such guises all have the aim of strengthening the reader's illusion that the narrated material is a part of his own experience of reality. "The aim of all narrative technique is none other than the creation of verisimilitude for the narrated material."[11] To be sure, Julius Petersen's proposition must be supplemented. For the reader of today this kind of guise often represents the game-like nature of fictional creation. It is a game with the reader's willingness to accept the fictional world from the standpoint of his own empirical reality. Even in this case the narrative guise is not necessarily an essential element of the novel. If necessary the reader can even do without it completely. These variations establish the conditions from which two main types of novel are derived—the authorial and the figural type. To these must be added a third type of equal rank—the first-person novel.

As we showed at the outset, many authors of today do not fully and consciously exploit the possibilities inherent in the novel for presenting a fictional world. Rather, they present the novel with demands and expectations which could be fulfilled far better by the nonfictional registration of reality in historical research, in sociology, and in anthropology. In such cases the narrative guise, which seeks to present the narrated material as a part of the reader's experience of reality, is taken in a literal sense which is inconsistent with the real purposes of literary creation. In order to clarify the unique nature of literary presentation ("literary" in the sense of the artistically successful), one must delve more deeply into the process of poetic presentation. In his book *Das literarische Kunstwerk* Roman Ingarden treats the adjacent realms of ontology, logic, and literary theory. His investigations will prove highly useful here.

One of the most common ambitions among authors of a realistic bent is to present "a picture of reality which is as unadulterated as possible." These authors may be more or less conscious of the impossibility of realizing such a goal in a literal sense. They may not be sufficiently aware, however, that as in other genres the novel's presentational capacity depends upon the presentational potential of language itself. Everywhere in the realm of literary art, moreover, there are innumerable places where subjective and personal elements can arise. In the reality of their experience, which many authors hope to reproduce without adulteration, all objects and processes are "generally and precisely fixed," that is, at no point and at no moment are they empty or unqualified. In a literary work, on the other hand, the objects presented manifest a large number of "indeterminate areas." Such a work always consists of a finite number of words; the infinitely manifold nature of an object's mode of existence can only be realized by means of high selectivity.[12] Every object presented in literature must thus remain a "schematic construct with various kinds of indeterminate areas."[13] This circumstance reveals a certain disadvantage in the literary presentation of an object, as compared to the real object. At the same time, however, it is precisely this schematization which offers the possibility of genuinely artistic formation. This more than compensates for the relative lack of definiteness of the fictional object. In the act of reading the imagination of the involved reader reendows the fictional object, despite numerous indeterminate areas, with sufficient general definiteness and unity. In such a "concretization"[14] of the literary work not only the discursive meaning of the individual words and sentences is transmitted into the reader's imagination; the potential for expression at the level of sounds and images in the work is also activated and thus affects the fictional world. To be sure, in the prose of the novel these two levels of the work—that of sounds and that of images and metaphors—only rarely reach the intensity inherent in metrical forms of literature. Their effect, however, is more strongly cumulative because of the large size of the novel and thus should not be overlooked completely. In truly great moments of narrative literature even individual pages can attain an intensity in sound and structure of meaning which approaches that of lyric poetry. Above all, however, interpreters of the novel must always focus on the manner in which the continuous unrolling of narrative strands creates a world in the reader's imagination. Such a world increases in definiteness with every word. The genesis of fictional reality occurs according to certain ordering patterns which are determined by the structure of the novel. Structure should be understood as the interaction, the interdependence, and the unity of all the elements which make up a novel. No attempt will be made to define this concept more precisely, for its content and range change with almost every work. Specific interpretations will serve to show which elements of a novel can be structurally determinative and the extent to which the knowledge of a novel's structure can be employed for its interpretation.

Notebooks and diaries show that most novelists choose the narrative situation and its guise quite consciously after carefully weighing the various formal possibilities available for their particular expressive purpose. On the other hand, structure is the result of a deliberate plan only to the extent that it is basically determined by the choice of the narrative situation. The final shape of the structure arises with the unique realization of this basic plan in the author's individual creative imagination, world view, experience of reality, perspective, and so forth. External factors, such as working method or serial publication, also affect substantially the final structure of a novel.

There are authors who believe themselves capable of registering the surrounding reality like a camera and reproducing it in their work. "I try to put down what I've seen, what I feel," says Danny O'Neill, a young writer in J. T. Farrell's novel *My Days of Anger* (p. 303). In extreme cases a catalogue of the fragmentary perceptions and experiences of the author is the result. Life with its innumerable false trails and cul-de-sacs, its often senselessly extravagant fullness, and its simultaneous meagreness and absurd narrowness is held by such authors to be in itself worthy of portrayal. Nevertheless, their novels can never become mirrors which merely reflect their vision of this chaos. Here the interpretative power inherent in the novel form is especially striking. Even rudimentary structural elements such as beginnings and endings, chapter divisions, selection of the fictional world by leaps in time and compression, choice of point of view, and so on, impose a structure of meaning on the fictional world. All this has an interpretative effect on the reader's imagination.

Complex structures with a high capability of interpretation, on the other hand, will appear when an author expends conscious effort in shaping his work. He then molds the experiences of life in their various manifestations, concatenations, phases, and the like into the regulated and complete whole which in life is only the exception. These artists differ from the first group above all in their conception of what is truly worthy of presentation. For them presentation is always synonymous with reshaping reality, with developing and revealing the structures of meaning which reality contains only in an obscure and confused state. Henry James assumed this position with complete consistency. For him the opposition of life and art formed the initial problem in his poetics of the novel:

> Life being all inclusion and confusion, and art being all discrimination and selection, . . . life persistently blunders and deviates, loses herself in the sand. The reason is of course that life has no direct sense whatever for the subject and is capable, luckily for us, of nothing but splendid waste.
>
> (Preface to *The Spoils of Poynton* in *Prefaces*, p. 120)

The structural meaning of fictional reality, says James, is more tautly, consistently, economically arranged than that of the real world, which drifts toward its goal along vast, rambling, confusing, and often intricate paths. The result of this is necessarily a concept of art which sees the "human and poetic" value of artistic presentation above all in the fulfillment of the general human desire to "intensify dynamically the dull and confused course of life, to order it rhythmically, to give it form."[15] More recently Albert Camus has described the author's task of presentation as a correction of the real world. "This correction which the artist undertakes by means of his language and by a redistribution of elements derived from reality is called style and gives the recreated universe its unity and its boundaries."[16] In the novel it is prominently the structure which serves to give the events order and rhythm, to correct formless reality.

The novels of Henry James, as one might expect, present very interesting problems in the formation of structure. One aspect of such a structure, James's method of concluding *The Portrait of a Lady*, will serve to illustrate the significance of the structure for a complete interpretation of the novel. The conclusion of James's novel can be compared to the keystone of an arch. Only when the keystone is in place is the external design of the arch complete. The parts then form a unity and the alternation of individual parts is revealed as the rhythm of the whole. For this reason deep caesuras in the action or marked intersections in the theme complex—such as marriage and death—are especially popular in forming the conclusion. In numerous picaresque novels the stereotypical conclusion with the marriage of the hero represents the norm. In the detective novel the end almost always signifies the discovery of the culprit. Both these forms are valid endings, for they correspond fully to the stereotypical patterns upon which these kinds of novel are constructed. In the case of the picaresque novel the episodes follow one after the other with increasing rapidity. The process ends at the point where intensification is no longer conceivable and where the receptivity of the reader is satiated. This series of episodes flows finally into a conclusion of complete rest. Such a conclusion may appear, from the point of view of the content, somewhat irrelevant, but in respect to the preceding movement it has a certain logical significance. The detective novel is brought to a close by tightening with a sudden jerk all the countless intertwining threads of discovery. The threads suddenly seem to draw together to a single point in surprising orderliness. A great novel only rarely makes use of such a conclusion. Some authors even exhibit a strong personal dislike for the traditional forms of conclusion. E. M. Forster, for example, once felt compelled to inveigh against "that idiotic use of marriage as a finale."[17] Frequently an unusual or unexpected conclusion becomes a challenge to survey the whole work once more from this vantage point; one must retrace the work's elements in detail with the final solution in view. Thus a decisive reason for the contradictory interpretations of the end of *The Portrait of a Lady* is partly to be found in the fact that the conclusion is not viewed as a component of the novel's unique structural plan. Whether Isabel Archer returns to her husband, even though their irreconcilable alienation has become clear, is a question which should not be answered as if she would then lead a life of resignation at the side of her husband. Such is the tenor of interpretations by F. O. Matthiessen, F. W. Dupee, Graham Greene, and several others.[18] James chose an open conclusion which does not clearly determine Isabel's future, for a look forward to the further development of the heroine could only have been rendered in simplified and compressed form. It would thus have disrupted the unity of the heroine's experience as it is presented in the novel. Ralph Touchett's death finally forces Isabel to recognize the complete failure of her ideals and expectations in the face of the reality of life. To present Isabel's life from this moment of recognition onward as a life of self-sacrifice with her husband Osmond would amount to a crude simplification. It would contradict the complex character relationships demonstrated in the novel. This kind of simplification —in its positive form as a "happy ending"—is certainly justifiable for the conclusion of the robust situations of the picaresque novel, where the author dispatches his figures into the meadows of everlasting, untroubled marital bliss. More than once Henry James expressed the view that unity and a closed structure have to be imprinted on the initial material of the work. Hence he found all stereotypical structural patterns suspect. In the preface to *Roderick Hudson* James writes:

> Where, for the complete expression of one's subject, does a particular relation stop—giving way to some other not concerned in that expression?
> Really, universally, relations stop nowhere, and the exquisite problem of the artist is eternally but to draw, by a geometry of his own, the circle within which they shall happily *appear* to do so.
> (*Prefaces*, p. 5)

James made several notes to *The Portrait of a Lady* when the greater part of the novel was complete and when approximately half had appeared in a magazine. He indicates without ambiguity the way he understood the conclusion of his novel:

> The obvious criticism of course will be that it is not finished—that I have not seen the heroine to the end of her situation—that I have left her *en l'air.*—This is both true and false. The *whole* of anything is never told; you can only take what groups together. What I have done has that unity—it groups together. It is complete in itself—and the rest may be taken up or not, later.
>
> (*Notebooks*, p. 18)

A smooth, definitive conclusion almost always excludes the possibility of a continuation. The conclusion of *The Portrait of a Lady* allows the possibility of a continuation of the novel—in a new, self-contained work, to be sure. James did seriously consider a continuation. The reason it was never written can be seen in the fact that the author soon felt himself alienated from the whole work.[19] The novel's structure of meaning, in his view, was not to be realized in Isabel's return to Osmond, but rather by the process of Isabel's awakening to the recognition that her ideal conceptions of life did not correspond to reality, that her life up to this point was completely misdirected. This conclusion is a very bitter one for the heroine; it excludes even an externally happy ending. Nevertheless, Isabel's recognition has positive significance, for here her life has reached a point of unambiguous meaning. From this point her past, too, no longer appears lost.

Day after day the reader is exposed to a great mass of semi-literary and subliterary products. This mass combines with novels of stereotypical structure to increase substantially the formation of presentational conventions. Reporting in newspapers and in radio as a rule recognizes only the law of usefulness in organization and presentation. An event or series of events is reported with consecutive chronology and usually with a constant degree of compression. This technique can be altered for purposes of expediency. The American newspaper is one example. On the front page an event is reported in extreme concision beneath a headline of appropriate size. On subsequent pages of the news-paper this portrayal is then repeated two or three times with the addition of further details. A certain principle of organization can be seen in the arrangement of facts according to their de-creasing news value or sensational quality. With this exception, however, such variation of the usual consecutive form of report-ing does not really provide a structure capable of interpretation. The structure is created exclusively for purposes of journalistic expediency. It does not arise from an intentional and interpreta-tive creative purpose. Yet just this kind of structure, in which an event is only fully portrayed by a series of tellings, can become a valid novel structure. Examples of such structures are to be found in William Faulkner's *The Sound and the Fury* and, employed in a quite different manner, in *Absalom, Absalom!* In this novel certain events are presented several times over—by clever manipulation of the narrative situation, by limitation of the point of view, and by disruption of the original temporal order of events. Only gradually does the reader recognize the proper position and significance of the events within the whole pattern of relationships.

In numerous novels the structure is as direct and functional in its arrangement as the news story of a European newspaper. In many cases this is ideally suited to the author's formative and expressive purpose. For this study, however, I have chosen novels whose structures represent true "physiognomies of the reflective process,"[20] since its purpose is to demonstrate the interpretability of novel structure. For reasons of method this study will distin-guish simply between novels with "imitative" structure, which are organized purely for expediency of presentation, and novels with "intentional structure," that is, with structure capable of in-terpretation.

The opposition of "imitative" and "intentional" as typical possibilities of novel structure purposely simplifies and isolates certain aspects of the novel. It has a certain parallel in Arnold Kettle's distinction between "life" and "pattern" as structural models.[21] "Life" is narrated with no apparent modification. No structurally determinative idea, no rule of life, no specific world view appears to take shape in the work. Here multiplicity of observation and detail, immediacy and vitality of the fictional world prevail. Usually there is a lack of a closed, ordering, interpretative structure of meaning as the formal expression of an idea. Kettle, with disarming theoretical insouciance, defines "pattern" as "the quality in a book which gives it wholeness and meaning, makes the reading of it a complete and satisfying experience. This is a matter partly, but only partly, discussable in terms used by the devotees of 'form.' "[22] Less from this definition than from his use of the concept of "pattern" it becomes evident that Kettle has in mind essential aspects of the "intentional" mode. Kettle also links the first flourishing of the "life" novel with the simultaneous development of journalism, as exemplified in the works of Defoe. This connection (which is not really new with Kettle) is instructive in view of the relationship between imitative novel structure and the stereotypical forms of presentation employed by the subliterary mass media.

E. M. Forster's *Aspects of the Novel* also treats various possibilities of artistic organization and various stages in forming the material. These distinctions refer in part to what is meant here by the imitative and intentional structural modes. For E. M. Forster the three concepts "story," "plot," and "pattern" represent three stages in the creation of a novel's structure of meaning. The first stage has the least measure of interpretability; the last the greatest. Forster also adds a fourth stage, "rhythm," but this is actually only a special aspect of "pattern." In the "story" the narration of an event is structurally determined by the reader's ever-present question: "And then?" Forster calls this "a very low form" of narrative art, "the chopped-off length of the tapeworm of time."[23] In his concept of "pattern" Forster comes very close to the idea of novel structure as an interpretable structure of meaning. Forster's examples express better than his definition what he means by "pattern." "Pattern" is a meaningful order in the total impression, a shape in the represented object which strives for comprehensive inclusiveness in the action. It can be best represented by some sort of picture or design. One of Forster's examples is of particular interest. For *The Ambassadors* Forster believes that the hourglass can best symbolize this "pattern." He shows in detail how the novel's action and characters, the revelation of relationships, the development of meaning from the start of narration to the conclusion and resolution—how all this seems to be part of a structure which can be portrayed in the form of an hourglass. Forster is fully aware of the merely pictorial, metaphorical nature of this explanation: "We just have a pleasure without knowing why, and when the pleasure is past, as it is now [after the reading!], and our minds are left free to explain it, a geometrical simile such as an hour-glass will be found helpful."[24] E. M. Forster's insights into the structural possibilities of the novel take the form of highly personal and intuitive statements, which, however, gain in importance because of his own successful career as a writer.

In his book *The Structure of the Novel* Edwin Muir proceeds from the three perceptional categories of time, space, and causality. Scholarship had until then severely neglected the first two categories. Muir establishes a correspondence between these three categories and three novel types. Each type is characterized by the predominance of one of the three categories: the dramatic novel, the character novel, and the chronicle.[25] As typical examples Muir cites among others: *Wuthering Heights, Vanity Fair,* and *War and Peace*. In this way Muir undeniably is able to reveal certain characteristic structural features of the fictional world. The value of his three novel types for the interpretation of individual works, however, remains small. On close observation almost every novel betrays the characteristics of all three novel types. These characteristics serve as elements which successively determine the structure of a given novel. On the other hand, these elements may interact in such a way that interpretative differentiation becomes impossible. At the basis of Muir's postulation of these three novel types apparently lies the idea that reality viewed as time, space, and causality can only be presented as a schematic construct. During fictional presentation time and space continually undergo disruption, which the reader counteracts in his mind. This process has been investigated in detail by Roman Ingarden.

A systematic typology of the novel, however, was only a part of Muir's purpose. It would be unfair to Muir to dismiss his numerous, highly enlightening insights into novelistic structure and presentation. For this investigation Muir's views on the question of structure are of special interest. He uses the expression "structure" frequently, but avoids a precise definition of the concept. It is quite evident that Muir is aware of certain aspects of the structural contrast between the imitative and intentional modes. This is apparent from a passage in which he recapitulates the purpose of his investigation:

> For the object of this argument is to show that the plot of the novel is as necessarily poetic or aesthetic as that of any other kind of imaginative creation. It will be an image of life, not a mere record of experience; but being an image it will inevitably observe the conditions which alone make the image complete and universal, and those, I have tried to show, reduce themselves to a representation of action predominantly in time or predominantly in space. (*The Structure of the Novel*, p. 149 f.)

The concluding chapter of this study, which attempts a new typology, will return to Muir's three novel types and Wolfgang Kayser's elaboration of them.

Günther Müller's treatment of novel structure employs a critical approach derived from Goethe's morphology. In the relationship of the duration of narrated material (*narrated time*) to the duration of the narrative process (*narrative time*) Müller discovers a very fruitful approach for the study of novel structure.[26] Among English critics A. A. Mendilow recently made the various aspects of time the basis of his study of the novel.[27] Günther Müller's approach is especially productive because he focuses on the fictional process as it projects itself in a line—both as the time of the narrated material and as the time of narration. It is precisely here that the creative process in the novel has decisive consequences which are specifically characteristic of the genre.

The manner in which this linear projection (Petsch distinguishes between linear projection, duration, and density)[28] is realized in the work reveals a highly important aspect of novel structure. Müller proposes the term *Zeitraffung* or *time compression* to describe the process of selection or schematization which occurs when a series of events is projected in time, that is, in a line. With the help of this concept Horst Oppel elucidates the structural principles and forms of the Victorian novel.[29] Günther Müller himself has investigated the temporal structures of a number of novels. He is concerned mainly with "isolating the course of events" by means of the concepts of narrative time and narrated time. For example, Müller regards the "unilinear life-curve" as the characteristic structure of the developmental novel:

> This form moves temporally like the hand of a clock, forward through years and even decades, presenting various milieus along with the progression of the developing self. Moreover, its development is characterized by a fundamentally unified meaning; it presents a curve-like course of events which can be surveyed as a whole.[30]

Once the typical nature of such a structure has been determined the individual structural qualities and variations of a given novel can be established by comparison with the typical structure. The establishment, however, of conclusive fundamental novel forms requires a large number of individual interpretations. This task is further complicated by novels which cannot immediately be assigned to one of the more obvious basic categories such as developmental novel, generation novel, picaresque novel, or detective novel.

D. H. Lawrence's novels *The Rainbow* and *Women in Love*, for example, do not belong to any immediately recognizable type. His novels present especially interesting problems of structure because he advocated a concept of art which does not allow any conscious formative effort beyond the spontaneous creative process. To be sure, this concept of art was for Lawrence himself an ideal of the creative process which he did not always succeed in realizing. The fact that he took it seriously, however, is evident in his sense of opposition to authors who followed Flaubert's model by striving for formal and stylistic perfection in their works. D. H. Lawrence felt that this concept of art had alienated Flaubert from life and that Flaubert "stood away from life as from a leprosy."[31] For this reason most of Lawrence's novels do not manifest that sort of structural symmetry and inclusiveness which can best be represented by a geometrical figure and which is almost always the result of well-planned and thoroughly reworked composition. Lawrence's letters show that these two novels grew out of what was originally planned as one work, *The Sisters*.[32] Even after finally completing the work in two novels Lawrence still insisted that they formed a single whole.[33] An interpretation of these two novels using Günther Müller's method reveals a highly instructive situation. The structure of the first novel is continued by the structure of the second. Only the end of the second novel brings the structure of the first to a conclusion. Lawrence's view of the two novels as a unit is confirmed by their structural pattern. The novels' structure is characterized by a series of critical high points which arise rhythmically from the action like wave crests. The themes of the novels grow out of the basic concern of all of D. H. Lawrence's works: "the inner war which is waged between people who love each other, a war out of which comes knowledge and . . . ."[34] It is significant that Lawrence breaks off his sentence here. Throughout his life he strove in his works to discover and express what is missing here. Any discursive statement of it would amount to falsification or simplification. In *The Rainbow* and *Women in Love* the confrontation with this problem has left its traces at the level of the novels' very structure.

In the pattern of the structure the wave crests represent culminating points, decisive critical moments in the struggle of man and woman to arrive at mutual understanding. D. H. Lawrence's characters can only approach this state through continuous alternation between violent attraction and repellent alienation. This rhythm of life is expressed structurally not in movement progressing toward a single denouement, but rather in the cumulative sequence of wave crest and wave trough. Before the point is reached when this rhythm of life between two figures fades away the figures always step out of the spotlight of presentation. They in turn become witnesses of the same struggle in the succeeding generation. In this way three generations pass before the reader—always in couples, in highly charged polarity: Tom Brangwen and Lydia Lensky; Will Brangwen and Anna; and finally, Ursula and Birkin with the contrasting couple Gudrun and Gerald. The structure of these two novels, however, does not form a unit merely because characters and themes of the first recur in the second. In the second novel the increasing violence of the struggle expresses itself in the shortening of the intervals between the wave crests of the structure. It is only in this second novel that the structure of meaning first manifested by Tom Brangwen and Lydia in *The Rainbow* assumes its unified, closed shape through the sudden conclusion in a wave trough. Thus the problems of the characters of the first novel must be viewed in the light of the knowledge and insight attained by later characters. Ursula and Birkin finally recognize that for their life together there can be no solution in a neat arithmetic sense. The only conceivable solution would be exhaustion.

Here a sequence of novels, which in content has much in common with the generation novel, has a quite individual structure. This unique novel structure demonstrates its artistic necessity by the fact that it follows and illustrates the inner movement of the fictional events. The unique course of inner development in Lawrence's two novels only becomes clear in comparison with the structure of the typical generation novel, in which above all the tendency toward decline and dissipation of strength emerges.

This brief indication of how the structure of two novels can be related to matters of content could be extended to the study of many other novels and to the comparison of their structure with that of the typical kinds of novels which are most closely related to them by form and content. In this investigation only a very limited area can be studied in detail. The individual interpretations propose to elucidate novel structure and hence the whole artistic organization of fictional presentation from a standpoint which has not received sufficient attention in the previous studies mentioned. Our starting point will be the concept of mediacy of presentation. Fictional mediacy manifests itself in the novel's narrative situation and in the specific narrative guise. The narrative situation determines the structure in two ways. It determines the order in which the narrator or author can unfold the fictional world before the eyes of the reader. At the same time the narrative situation and its specific guise bring the reader to expect a definite consistency of illusion from the narrative. The narrator or author must conform to this "illusion expectancy." As a result characteristic narrative conventions are formed for each narrative situation. Such conventions receive approbation through a tacit agreement between author and reader. Throughout the following study a double perspective will be employed as far as possible without subjecting the interpretations to an overly rigid schematism. The structurally determinative elements of the novel are viewed first from the standpoint of the author— presentation, mediation, interpretation—and secondly from the standpoint of the reader—reception, imagination, concretization.

The next chapter, which precedes the specific interpretations, outlines more sharply the basis of this study and provides definitions of several indispensable concepts. This discussion also clarifies the principle upon which the following chapters are arranged. Important works of English and American literature have been chosen for the individual interpretations. Preference has been given to novels with a multiplicity of relevant structural features rather than to clear, unified examples of a given type. Several of the individual interpretations are preceded by a discussion of the type of novel represented there. The four individual interpretations are followed by an excursus on the ways of rendering consciousness in the novel. The last chapter attempts finally to outline a typology of the novel based on the conclusions of the preceding chapters.

I

THE NARRATIVE SITUATION AND

THE EPIC PRETERITE

Since otto ludwig contrasted true narration with scenic narration in his essay "Formen der Erzählung"[1] the critical and creative treatment of these concepts has not died down. This circumstance leads us to take up these two concepts once again in order to develop them from the standpoint of this study. This is naturally not the place to treat the—at times highly polemical —attempts of Friedrich Spielhagen and other critics and authors who have tried to establish exclusive validity for scenic narrative.[2] The lasting repercussions of Otto Ludwig's categories prove that his forms of narration (he also names a third form in which the other two forms are united) are valid types of narrative which preclude any normative claims by one of the three types. In order to avoid the confusion of concepts which has evolved since his essay, Ludwig's true narration will be called "reportlike narration"; his scenic narration will be called "scenic presentation."

Otto Ludwig already saw that each type of narration tends to present a certain kind of material and relationships. He found, for example, that reportlike narration is well suited to present gradual change, development, and certain processes which only become truly meaningful when they are illuminated by the imagination of the author or when explained and interpreted by him. Scenic presentation, on the other hand, is less abstract in nature, according to Ludwig. It projects the action directly before the eyes of the reader and concentrates it both in space and in time. In reportlike narration, says Ludwig, the original sequence of events can only be disrupted by the intrusion of the author, while in scenic presentation it is possible to suspend the original chronology and to arrange events from the point of view of tension, ideal order, contrast, and so forth.

All of Ludwig's observations concerning the two kinds of narration can be reduced to one basic difference—the author's presence in or absence from the narrative. Presence and absence are not taken here in the epistemological sense, that is, as a question of the existence of the author. They refer to the author's visibility in the narrative or to his withdrawal behind the fictional world. Presence of the author means that the narrator and the narrative process take on a definite shape in the reader's imagination in addition to the narrated events. In this case reportlike narration usually predominates. In the case of predominantly scenic narration, on the other hand, the image of the narrator is not evoked in the mind of the reader. It is thus already evident that the mode of narration and the corresponding presence or absence of the author in the narrative have a decisive effect on the reader's imagination. Inasmuch as the presence or absence of the author in the reader's imagination can only be known approximately, it is more useful to speak of the author either emerging or withdrawing in the course of narration. If the author emerges by addressing the reader, by commenting on the action, by reflections, etc., the reader will bridge the gap between his own world and fictional reality under the guidance, so to speak, of the author. This is *authorial* narration. If the reader has the illusion of being present on the scene in one of the figures, then *figural* narration is taking place. If the point of observation does not lie in any of the novel's figures, although the perspective gives the reader the feeling of being present as an imaginary witness of the events, then the presentation can be called *neutral*.

In an authorial narrative the author-narrator portrays himself in addition to the action. He remains, however, for the most part outside the realm of the fictional world. Occasionally the guise of the narrator as chonicler, editor of an autobiography or diary, etc., requires that the author establish some connection with the fictional world. This relationship is seldom developed further in the narrative, for it endangers the freedom of the authorial narrator. The authorial narrator strives for sovereign independence from his fictional world and for temporal, spatial, and psychological distance from it. This narrative distance is an important characteristic of the authorial narrative situation. For Emil Staiger this spatio-temporal distancing of the narrator from the narrative is the essential element of the epical mode.[3] This view was developed chiefly with the Homeric epic in mind and is valid for this form of the epical mode. It is also valid for the authorial novel, which has a narrative situation very similar to that of the Homeric epic. As will be shown, however, this narrative distance can be completely suspended in another type of novel. When the reader can clearly recognize the narrative distance in a novel his attention is divided between two realms—the realm of the author, in which the narrative process takes place, and the fictional world, in which the narrated action occurs. The characteristic structure of meaning in the authorial novel finds its basic tension in this polarity. In addition to the narrated action and the characters, then, one must interpret above all the specific manifestation of the authorial narrator, the idiosyncracy of his world view, and his fictional disguises and metamorphoses.

Interpreters of the novel frequently overlook the fact that the figure of the authorial narrator is not simply identical with the personality of the author. Several critics have remarked on the differences—to be sure often quite subtle—between the actual author and his narrator-figure.[4] In order to distinguish the specific nature of the narrator-figure more sharply from the personality of the actual author the term *authorial medium* will be used in this study. This term combines all those aspects of the authorial narrator which can be discerned as the narrator forms himself in the process of narration. The authorial medium must also be distinguished from the *figural medium*, which must always be a figure of the novel through whose eyes the reader seems to view the fictional world.

"Authorial" and "figural" thus designate the two typical possibilities of employing the novel's mediacy of presentation for narrative purposes. Between these two typical possibilities of presentation lies the first-person form of the novel. This form, as will be shown, has both authorial and figural capabilities. In an authorial narrative situation the mediacy of narration is, as it were, dramatized: the author, in the figure of the authorial medium, takes up a definite stance toward the narrative. In the figural narrative situation the narrator withdraws; the mediacy of presentation is concealed from the reader. The realization of a figural narrative situation in the reader's imagination is in this respect similar to the realization of a staged drama in the imagination of the audience.

Depending on the origins and nature of their systems, theoreticians of the narrative have assumed quite varied positions on the question of the mode of narration. In opposition to Friedrich Spielhagen's exaggerated demands for "objectivity," i.e., for the complete disappearance of the figure of the narrator, Käte Friedemann's book *Die Rolle des Erzählers in der Epik* (1910) endeavors to reestablish the legitimacy of authorial narration. Friedemann, to be sure, commits the same error as Spielhagen— this time in the other extreme. She sees the essence of epic presentation exclusively in the "self-manifestation of a narrator."[5] While Spielhagen recognized only the figural or neutral narrative situation, Friedemann limits the forms and creative possibilities of the novel to the authorial narrative situation. Both views are too exclusive to be tenable. Robert Petsch, approaching the problem from his analysis of "basic epic forms," attributes the greatest epic effectiveness to the report or to reportlike narration. The epic scene or scenic presentation, he says, can be only a "weak copy" of the dramatic scene.[6] In contrast to Petsch, Otto Ludwig believes that scenic presentation is richer in creative possibilities than the reportlike narrative and even than the drama. The author who makes use of scenic presentation can do "all that thought can do; there is no effective limit to his presentation; there is no physical impossibility for his scene; he can do all that nature and the mind can do."[7] Similarly, Percy Lubbock tends to see the high point of narrative creativity in the later novels of Henry James, where scenic presentation predominates.[8] Käte Friedemann and Robert Petsch developed their sense of form primarily from the novel of the nineteenth century, which normally had a preference for the authorial narrative situation (Thackeray and Wilhelm Raabe). This sense of form was necessarily alien to the attempts of authors of the twentieth century to make consistent use of scenic presentation even in long narratives. Petsch went so far as to call the novels of James Joyce, Dos Passos, and Alfred Döblin the cultivation of a "form of nonform."[9] In recent decades, however, the so-called objective or dramatic novel, the novel with a figural or neutral narrative situation, has come to the fore. In 1915 Oskar Walzel had already detected a reorientation of the reading public away from predominantly reportlike narration and toward scenic presentation:

> We have, however, become so accustomed to the technique of the scenic novel that we have more difficulty reading works in which dialogue does not predominate, where the narrator narrates and for the most part allows his figures to speak only in indirect discourse. Since Otto Ludwig's time the tide has turned completely. He could still speak of the difficulties of experiencing events which appear in the dramatic form of narration. We have more difficulty today when quotation marks are used only sparingly, when instead of the short paragraphs of the dialogue the longer paragraphs of pure narration appear before the eye.
>
> (*Das Wortkunstwerk*, p. 198)

This observation is corroborated by Joseph Warren Beach's book, *The Twentieth Century Novel*, in which the introductory chapter is significantly entitled "Exit Author."

Despite the fact that this tendency to scenic presentation is so strong there can be no doubt that the authorial narrative situation continues to enjoy great popularity beside the figural and neutral types. It is high time, however, that the theory of the novel come to terms with this fact and renounce once and for all the normative valuation of specific types of narration or novel forms. Such a valuation is still to be heard in the postscript which Oskar Walzel gives to his book in 1925. He greets the appearance of Thomas Mann's *Zauberberg* as a healthy return of the modern novel to the narrative of sovereign authorial report and authorial intrusion.[10] Recently Wolfgang Kayser attributed a certain literary superiority to the authorial novel. We will return to his article "Die Anfänge des modernen Romans im 18. Jahrhundert und seine heutige Krise" in a later context.

In the present study the authorial novel and the figural novel (with its variant, the neutral figural novel or objective novel) are viewed as fully equal manifestations of the genre. Together with the first-person novel and its variant, the epistolary novel, these forms represent typical creative possibilities of the novel form; from them all other forms can be derived.

In an authorial novel all power of illusion and order seems to emanate from the author's presence in the figure of the authorial narrator. By changing this fictional guise and varying his appearance as narrator the author is able to realize his mediative capacity. He can introduce himself into the mind of the reader in the most varied manners and shapes. This metamorphosis of the author into an authorial medium; the recognizable designation of the narrative distance and thus the predominance of the report; and finally the continuous guiding, directorlike, interpretative intrusion of the narrator into the story—these are the characteristic marks of the authorial novel. They also serve to determine largely the imaginative process of the reader and his spatio-temporal orientation in the fictional world. They call attention to the presence of the narrator, his now-and-here in the act of narration. The reader takes this now-and-here of the narrator for the basis of his spatio-temporal orientation in the fictional world. The point which is spatially and temporally fixed in this way in the reader's imagination will be called the reader's center of orientation. In the case of the authorial narrative situation the center of orientation is always identical with the now-and-here of the author in the act of narration.[11] Using an abbreviation of

Bühler's concept of the "Origo des Jetzt-Hier-Ich-Systems," Käte Hamburger calls this point the "Ich-Origo" of the communicating, experiencing being or of a character in the narrative.[12]

In a presentation with a figural narrative situation the power to create illusion and order, to interpret the world originates in a figure of the novel, the figural medium. In this way the reader's center of orientation, too, is located in the now-and-here of the figure. The reader identifies with this figure and assumes the temporal and spatial organization of its experience. Neutral presentation, which is a special case of figural presentation, occurs when the perspective of observation is not fixed in any of the figures. This manner of presentation is seldom used alone in long narratives. It usually appears joined with a figural and sometimes even an authorial narrative situation. A passage presented in this way is also called an objective scene. Long passages of dialogue in which the act of speaking is seldom noted are often experienced by the reader as objective scenes. Here the reader's center of orientation lies in the scene itself, the now-and-here of a moment of the action. It could also be said that the center of orientation lies in the now-and-here of an imaginary observer on the scene whose place the reader assumes in his imagination.

In a passage with an authorial narrative situation the cross section through the process of mediation appears as follows: reader (expectation)—authorial narrator (his now-and-here in the act of narration; narrative preliminaries)—fictional reality (action experienced from the spatio-temporal standpoint of the narrator)—authorial narrator (his now-and-here in the act of narration; commentary on the action)—reader (image with the action colored by authorial interpretation). As a result the reader in an authorial narrative situation always envisions fictional reality from the narrator's spatio-temporal point of view and colored by authorial interpretation. The structure of meaning of an authorial novel is thus constructed mainly from the references and relationships between the fictional world and the figure of the authorial narrator and from the resulting tensions in values, judgments, and kinds of experience.

In a passage with a figural narrative situation, on the other hand, the process of mediation can be analyzed in the following manner: reader (expectation)—figure of the novel as figural medium (its now-and-here at a given moment of the action; the fictional world as the contents of its consciousness)—reader (in his imagination the fictional world appears as it is mirrored in the figural medium, together with the impression which the personality of this medium makes on the reader). In an objective scene or in a passage presented neutrally the clearly characterized personality of the figural medium is absent. The action appears to enter the reader's imagination without any subjective distortion or interpretation. Strictly speaking, of course, this objectivity is illusory, as we showed in our introductory discussion of the limits of objective creation in the novel.

The comparison of these three possibilities of conveying fictional reality to the reader's imagination clearly indicates that an interpreter of fiction must pay particular attention to the narrative situation. The narrative situation can reveal the angle, the bias, and the kinds of references and relationships through which the narrated material is presented to the reader. The work's general orientation, which is not without influence on the reader's imagination, is also determined by the narrative situation. A caveat, however, must immediately be attached to this neat differentiation of three kinds of mediation. Even when the narrative situation of a passage clearly proves to be authorial or figural, the imaginative process in the individual reader is by no means fixed with absolute certainty. The imaginative process of the individual reader encompasses a number of imponderables which can only be approximately by a description of typical reader attitudes. These typical attitudes will vary according to the sensitivity with which the individual reader is able to distinguish between the various possible narrative situations. A reader's sensitivity will depend on his ability to see a given narrative element as characteristic of reportlike narration or of scenic presentation. For the purposes of this study it will suffice in general to distinguish between two main types of readers.

The first type is characterized by the gift of and tendency toward intensive, scenic-dramatic imagination of the narrative at any given moment. This type of reader employs most of his imaginative energy in the full, pictorial, and detailed realization of the scene portrayed. Since the image of the scene immediately following is captured with similar pictorial concentration, the previous image must be suppressed or effaced again just as rapidly. Ultimately the old image is fully extinguished under the impression of the new one.

The second type of reader achieves a lower degree of pictorial intensity. Rather, he lends in his mind such perseverence to the main aspects of earlier material that the consecutive narrative is concentrated into a state of coexistence; this is seldom possible for the first type of reader. In addition the two types of reader differ in the interest with which they encounter certain novels. The first type evinces a preference for "exciting" novels, i.e., those which rush from one phase of the action to the next. The other type prefers novels where the action progresses more slowly, and with clear lines of development, with a rich interconnection of relationships. The types of reader characterized here illustrate, as it were, the extreme border cases between which the great mass of readers can be classified. In relation to the narrative situation of a novel the two types differ in the following ways. The first reader will generally accustom himself quickly to a change in the narrative situation. He will, for example, effortlessly relocate his center of orientation in the transition from the authorial report of a prehistory to a passage presented scenically; he readily moves away from the now-and-here of the reporting narrator and into the portrayal of a scene. After a few sentences of scenic presentation, when there is no longer any allusion to the narrator and the narrative process, he will already have forgotten the initial and fundamental presence of a narrator. In this case he no longer senses any "narrating," for the action appears directly present before his eyes. The other type of reader allows the original narrative situation to continue to affect his imagination. For him the passage with scenic presentation still appears as the vividly dramatized narration of the authorial medium, even after several pages. If some authorial intrusion then appears in the text, perhaps only in the form of a subjectively selected epithet, this will be sufficient to give new strength to the authorial narrative situation. In this way it is possible that the center of orientation may never shift from the now-and-here of the narrator. The whole context of narration, despite passages of scenic presentation, will be experienced as an authorial report. In the case of the first type of reader, on the other hand, it is difficult to fix the point at which this reader loses the impression of the original narrative situation and adjusts to the new one. A change of narrative situation in the reverse direction is, of course, also possible. The scenic presentation of a phase of the action may be followed by a more tightly compressed report. Here the first reader will transfer the narrative situation of scenic presentation over to the more highly compressed report. The second type will immediately recognize the authorial element present in the greater degree of compression. He will incorporate the presence of a narrator into his imagined world. In this way he registers a change in the narrative situation, while the first reader will not perceive this change.

In the following interpretations of individual novels the reader's dependency on the location and nature of the center of orientation will be described more thoroughly. Here we shall restrict our discussion to the importance of the center of orientation for determining the temporal relationships between fictional reality and the imaginative process of the reader. The circumstances which characterize authorial and figural mediation also provide an answer to the question of when the reader experiences the narrative events as something past and when he experiences them as present.

Robert Petsch, taking the report as the basic form of narration, unwittingly touches upon the problematic nature of this question. At one point he views the "unbridgable opposition between a distant time in the past and the present moment from which we view that time and find it meaningful," as the central concern of all epic presentation. On the very next page, however, he must add that the narrator constructs with the form of the epic preterite an "epic presence by means of his enrapturing, intensified senses."[13] In addition, says Petsch, the preterite is considered the true epic tense not only because of its past-time content, but also because it creates the "as if" illusion of narration which lends the narrated material "a validity which extends far beyond the present moment." Similarly Wolfgang Kayser attempts to derive "the structural elements of the epic world" from the "archtypal epic situation": "a narrator tells some listeners what has happened." In correspondence to this archtypal epic situation the narrative appears as something past. Yet Kayser, too, accepts the possibility of creating the effect of presentness in past material. He admits the possibility of a narrator who stands on a level with the action.[14] Julius Petersen basically follows the well-known distinction made by Goethe and Schiller (in their correspondence, December 1797): the dramatist presents events as present, the epic poet presents them as past. Petersen thus defines the epic (and the novel) as monologic report and the drama as the dialogic presentation of an event. But for Petersen the area between these two genres is replete with transitional forms such as the first-person narrative, the frame tale, the epistolary novel, the dialogue novel, and the dramatic portrait. These forms ascend in this order toward a stronger and stronger effect of presentness. This arrangement of the various forms will be criticized in the final chapter. Most important here is Petersen's belief that the basic type of narrative poetry presents the events as something past. The illusion of presentness in fiction is seen as a variant of this basic type. That Petersen, too, views the reportlike form of narration as the true form is evident from the fact that he calls consistent scenic presentation a "violation [sic] of the report form caused by the exclusion of the narrator."[15] Emil Staiger is of the opinion that the lyric poet descends into the past in memory, while the epic poet recollects the past. "And in this recollection the temporal as well as the spatial distance is retained."[16] Here one must consider that Staiger defines the epical mode almost exclusively with respect to the Homeric epic, where an authorial narrative situation predominates throughout. Nevertheless, even Staiger cannot help but allow the epic poet the possibility of creating the effect of presentness in the narrated material. At the same time he leaves it open whether the reader, too can repeat this creation of presentness in his imagination:

> What the lyric poet recalls, the epic poet makes present. Which is to say, he assumes a position on a level with life, no matter what date it may bear. Whether he is narrating the Fall of Adam and Eve or the Last Judgement, he puts everything before our eyes as if he had seen it himself.[17]

Untroubled by questions of genre theory, Joseph Warren Beach hits upon an apparent contradiction: in narration, to be sure, everything is set forth as past, but the reader frequently experiences the narrative as present in his imagination. This creation of presentness occurs, according to Beach, when the reader comes upon a "constituted scene." The expression, derived from the terminology of Henry James, refers to a passage in scenic presentation:

> In a story we have the psychological equivalent of the dramatic present whenever we have a vividly "constituted scene" . . . it is this which cheats the imagination, and persuades the reader that he is actually present, as a spectator, nay, perhaps as an actor in the drama.   (*The Twentieth Century Novel*, p. 148)

A. A. Mendilow also recognizes the possibility of creating the effect of presentness in material which is narrated as past:

> Mostly the past tense in which the events are narrated is transposed by the reader into a fictive present, while any expository matter is felt as a past in relation to that present.
>
> (*Time and the Novel*, p. 94)

According to Mendilow, then, the reader is able to create the effect of presentness beginning at that point in the narrative where he succeeds in shifting his center of orientation into the now-and-here of the fictional scene. This view becomes quite evident in Mendilow's further discussion of this question:

> There is as a rule one point of time in the story which serves as the point of reference. From this point the fictive present may be considered as beginning. In other words, the reader if he is engrossed in his reading translates all that happens from this moment of time into an imaginative present of his own and yields to the illusion that he is himself participating in the action or situation, or at least is witnessing it as happening, not merely as having happened. (*Time and the Novel*, pp. 96–97)

On the basis of an ontology of the literary work and the reality presented there Roman Ingarden attempts to meet this problem by indicating the quasi-real mode of existence of the reality presented in a literary work. This reality, he says, only represents an analogue to the reality of the reader. The fact that narrated events are "mainly presented in the light of the past" is for him above all the semantic expression of the ontic difference between the fictional and the real world. Ingarden, too, notes the importance of the various kinds of narration for the reader's temporal orientation. In the "summary" mode of narration, by which he apparently means a highly compressed reportlike novel, the narrated periods of time are always understood as past. Conversely the "zero-point of temporal orientation" shifts into the past when the phases of the action are given in their entire concrete fullness, that is, in a kind of scenic presentation. But as soon as the zero-point of the reader's orientation lies in the past, the narrated matter must appear to him as present. All told, Ingarden distinguishes three possible positions for the center of orientation. It can lie, he says, in the narrating author; in the fictional world, without being expressly fixed in one of the figures of the novel; or finally in one of the fictional figures.[18]

Recently Käte Hamburger narrowed this question to a discussion of the imaginative value of the epic preterite. Consciously avoiding the compromises and ambiguities of all these views, she reaches an original—if not fully valid—solution:

> The facts set forth in the novel are not narrated as past, but rather as present—as present for the narrator and reader who are mentally submerged in them. The past mode here only has the function of labelling the "world" of the narrative as a nonreal, *fictive* world and hence as a world which exists exclusively in the mode of imagination.[19]

The difficulties of such an explanation, which barely takes into account the narrative situation, are clear in the case of the first-person narrative. In her second article, Hamburger must exclude the first-person narrative from her formula as being "nonfictive."[20] Hamburger shows the difference between real and fictive in a statement about Mr. X: "He was in America." If this statement occurs in a conversation between two real people who are conversing about a third real person, it designates a real, a historical fact. The preterite of the statement stands for a real past-tense relationship. In the context of a novel, says Hamburger, the same statement would designate a fictive event, but one to be imagined as present. Mr. X is now, at this point in the action of the novel, in America; the reader imagines Mr. X in this situation now, that is, at present. In reference to this statement in a novel it would make no sense to ask, says Hamburger, when or how long Mr. X was in America. On the other hand the same question in the context of a conversation between real people would be quite meaningful.[21] Hamburger has unquestionably indicated an important difference between a real, historical circumstance and a literarily presented, fictive circumstance. For Hamburger, however, it seems to make no difference whether the statement about Mr. X appears in the context of a reportlike narrative or in scenic presentation. Only in a first-person narrative would the fictive mode and the imaginative meaning of the present fail to apply to the epic preterite. The difference between the narrative situation of the authorial and the figural novel is not taken into consideration. With Hamburger's example it is not difficult to illustrate the importance of the narrative situation in understanding the imaginative value of the epic preterite. Let the statement "Mr. X was in America" stand in a passage with predominating reportlike narration, perhaps directly following an allusion to the narrative presence of the authorial narrator. In this case the question, directed by the reader to the narrator, of when or how long Mr. X was in America, is quite conceivable. But if such a question is possible, then the statement about Mr. X can only have been understood by the reader as something past. If one now imagines the same statement "Mr. X was in America" in a novel with consistent figural or neutral presentation, the question of the time and length of his stay there is meaningless. Now the statement "Mr. X was in America" forms a part of the contents of a figure's consciousness. For this figure and thus for the reader whose center of orientation lies in this figure, the past statement has the imaginative value: "Mr. X is in America." For this case Käte Hamburger's explanation of the epic preterite is applicable; it now has the imaginative value of the present.*

The temporal orientation of the reader's imagination and the specific imaginative value of the epic preterite can only be determined from the context of all the structural elements in the narrative situation. The location of the reader's center of orientation is decisive for this temporal orientation. If the center lies in the now-and-here of the authorial narrator, as is the case in the authorial narrative situation and in predominating reportlike narration, the narrated matter will be realized in the reader's imagination as something past. The narrator enters the reader's imagination as the source of the narrative; his posteriority to the narrated material is transferred to the reader's imagination as a perspective of retrospection. Here the epic preterite is the expression of the past. On the other hand, the reader's center of orientation can lie in the consciousness of a figure or in an imaginary

* Subsequent to the articles discussed here Käte Hamburger presented and expanded upon her position in book form, *Die Logik der Dichtung* (1957; substantially revised edition, 1968), where she also replies to Stanzel's objections. An English translation of this work is forthcoming from Indiana University Press.—Translator's note.

observer on the scene of the fictional action, as in a figural or neutral narrative situation. In this case the action presented can be realized in the reader's imagination as present. Here the epic preterite can have the imaginative value of the present. One qualification must be added. The definition of the narrative situation indicates only the most probable orientation of a potential reader. The specific orientation of a given reader will depend on his own manner of reading and imagining.

II

THE AUTHORIAL NOVEL:

TOM JONES

THE AUTHORIAL NOVEL is narrated in the third person. The author himself seems to enter as narrator. From this narrative situation the reader derives his expectation of certain kinds of illusion. In order to meet this illusion expectancy; or to circumvent it without the reader's notice; or in order to play with it artistically, authors have varied, concealed, or disguised the authorial narrative situation in numerous ways.

In contrast to the first-person narrator, the typical authorial narrator stands outside the realm of existence of the fictional world. The authorial narrator may appear transformed or disguised as the editor of a manuscript, or as the reporter and chronicler of an event supposedly communicated to him by an eyewitness or participant, and so forth. To be sure, this kind of disguise outwardly forms a bridge from the authorial realm to the fictional world, but as a rule these two realms never come so close together that the action taking place in the fictional world could encroach on the authorial realm. The Romantic novel's playful urge to exchange or intermingle the various realms of reality is a special case. In many respects it actually helps reveal the basic properties of the typical novel forms. This playful upsetting of the illusion of the narrative situation can be found long before the Romantic novel. At least as far back as *Don Quixote* there are clear tendencies in this direction. From such play the strict forms of the novel have often received fruitful impulses toward extending their means of presentation.

The separation of the two realms of reality in the typical authorial novel enables the authorial narrator to assume a position of superiority over his figures. This superiority is either explained or concealed by the outer guise of the narrative situation (the narrator appears as chronicler, as editor, etc.). Only seldom does the narrator of the authorial novel reveal himself to the reader in the full creative arbitrariness and freedom which are really his rights as author. He wants the reader to understand his presentation not as an invented, but as a "real" world. The narrative spirit more popular in earlier periods, "se non è vero, è ben trovato," is now almost completely alien to the novel. The sudden flash, the inspiration, the happy thought of the inventive author is—as a stated source—unknown to the modern novel. The closest approximation has been taken over from medieval literature—the dream. It was still employed by Bunyan in *The Pilgrim's Progress*, but today it, too, has become very rare or is used only for parts and smaller sections of a novel. The guise of the narrative process is not always taken so seriously as to eliminate every trace of the original free rein of the author. It is no coincidence that the most carefree of all authorial narrators, Anthony Trollope, often veils but thinly his authorial pleasure at holding sovereign and arbitrary power over his own creatures. What else but the power of the author is concealed with irony in the word "destined" in the following passage from *Barchester Towers*:

> "Then, in God's name, let him marry Mrs. Bold," said Madeline. And so it was settled between them.
> But let the gentle-hearted reader be under no apprehension whatsoever. It is not destined that Eleanor shall marry Mr. Slope or Bertie Stanhope. (vol. 1, p. 180)

In his early essay "The Art of Fiction" Henry James condemned Trollope for his careless habit of occasionally telling the reader that "he and this trusting friend are only 'making belief.' "[1] For

James, who saw the high task of the novel in the fact "that it does compete with life,"[2] Trollope's narrative stance had to appear an almost frivolous misuse of the form. James did not intend a direct imitation or reproduction of reality in the sense of an objective historical presentation. This is quite clear from his later prefaces written for the New York Edition of his novels. To compete with reality in the presentation of life means for him to supplement reality—if need be with a possible, conceivable, but nowhere realized form or phenomenon of life. This creative supplementation of real life is equivalent to correcting reality from the viewpoint of the author's conception of the world and man. James's characters, which he himself called his "supersubtle fry,"[3] have often given rise to the criticism that they are too thoroughly sensitive and subtle to be found anywhere in reality. In his preface to *The Lesson of the Master* James quotes his own reply to a friend who had voiced this very criticism of his works. In this reply he speaks quite revealingly about his concept of art and the true task of the creative imagination:

"If the life about us for the last thirty years refuses warrant for these examples [his supersubtle fry], then so much the worse for that life. The *constatation* would be so deplorable that instead of making it we must dodge it: there are decencies that in the name of the general self-respect we must take for granted, there's a kind of rudimentary intellectual honour to which we must, in the interest of civilization, at least pretend." But I must really reproduce the whole passion of my retort.

"What does your contention of non-existent conscious *exposures*, in the midst of all the stupidity and vulgarity and hypocrisy imply, but that we have been, nationally, so to speak, graced with no instance of recorded sensibility fine enough to react against these things?—an admission too distressing. What one would accordingly fain do is to baffle any such calamity, to *create* the record, in default of any other enjoyment of it; to imagine, in a word, the honourable, the producible case. What better example than this of the high and helpful public and, as it were, civic use of the imagination?—a faculty for the possible employments of which in the interest of morality my esteem grows every hour I live." (*Prefaces*, pp. 222–23)

Although James could not accept Trollope's apparently careless use of his creative freedom and arbitrariness, he himself constantly fell back on this freedom and with its help escaped the dictates of reality, which he, too, found insufficient. Yet James's concept of the "civic use of the imagination" does seem irreconcilable with the view which Arnold Bennett, in particular, tried to realize in his works and criticism: "First-class fiction is, and must be, in the final resort autobiographical."[4] This view limits the truly creative element in the work of the author to the mere achievement of expression. The play between authorial free rein and apparent denial of this freedom through the specific guise of the narrative process—the decisive characteristic of the narrative situation of the authorial novel—becomes impossible if the author accepts Bennett's position.

In the authorial novel the separation between the authorial realm and fictional reality is retained in the guise of the act of narration. Henry Fielding's novel *Tom Jones*, which is a typical authorial novel, clearly displays these relationships. The narrator of *Tom Jones* rises far above the fictional reality in his essayistic sections, only to appear again immediately thereafter in the role of a chronicler who must assemble the facts of his history with laborious effort: ". . . we have taken uncommon pains to inform ourselves of the real fact. . . ."[5] This guise of the authorial narrative process was very popular during the real flowering period of the authorial novel in the eighteenth and nineteenth centuries. It appears to correspond best to the reader's main illusion expectancy in the authorial narrative situation—that the narrated material must be presented as actually having taken place. This illusion expectancy already discounts the imagination and the sudden flash of inspiration as sources of the narrated material. The fictional world claims to be a part of the real world or its historically verifiable copy. In his mediative position the authorial narrator is viewed as a guarantor of the authenticity and truth (meaning that which can be documented) of the narrated material. Nevertheless, Fielding is very sparing in contriving relationships between the authorial narrator of *Tom Jones* and the figures of the novel. This sparing attitude is characteristic of the authorial narrative situation, which despite all guises is always conscious of the separation between the realms of existence of the narrator and the narrated. In Fielding's earlier novel, *Joseph Andrews*, this separation is not maintained quite as strictly, for Parson Adams appears at one point as the immediate informant of the narrator. But even here this connection of the narrator to his figure is not expanded.[6] In the Romantic novel, which makes a game of upsetting illusion by intermingling the realms of existence, the two realms are sometimes placed on the same level. Clemens Brentano's *Godwi oder das steinerne Bild der Mutter* is an instructive example. The realm of the figures of the novel breaks into that of the author. Numerous meetings take place between the figures and the author; there are even discussions about the novel and its continuation. The same sort of thing can already be found in *Don Quixote*, where the title hero meets a man in the second volume who has already read the first volume of the novel.[7] The more numerous such contacts and relationships between the narrator and the novel's figures become, the further the narrator himself will be drawn into the realm of existence of the figures. This variation of the authorial narrative situation can ultimately lead to the narrative situation of the first-person novel, in which the narrator always appears as a figure of the fictional world. This borderline position between the authorial novel and the first-person novel is assumed not only by the Romantic novel. In another manner and with no intention of upsetting illusion Thackeray realized this middle position, which allows the author to shift now to the authorial narrative situation, now to the situation of the first-person novel. In his novel *The History of Henry Esmond Written by Himself* the narrator appears as the writer of his own biography. Although as a rule the narrator narrates about himself in the third person, one cannot view this novel simply as an authorial novel. The fact that the narrator and the main figure are identical is really a characteristic of the first-person narrative situation. The narrator of *Henry Esmond* also resorts to the "I" form upon occasion. For this reason the novel will be treated in more detail in the chapter on the first-person novel. It is mentioned here in order to show that a narrative situation can also be realized which lies between the typical authorial situation and that of the typical first-person novel. The authorial third-person novel and the first-person novel thus by no means represent forms fully isolated from one another. They allow variations of the two typical narrative situations from one type in the direction of the other. It can be noted here, however, that the borderline position of *Henry Esmond* is much less often realized than the typical narrative situations—the clearly authorial and the clearly first person.

Narrative distance is the next problem of the authorial narrative situation. This distance arises from fact that the authorial narrator stands in a relationship of posteriority to the narrated material. Whenever the authorial narrator relates something, he narrates what is past. The significance of this circumstance for the orientation of the novel and for the imaginative value of the epic preterite was discussed in detail in the first chapter. Narrative distance refers to the temporal remove which in the guise of the narrative act separates this act from the narrated event.[8] The narrative distance can be concretized in the reader's imagination in various ways and with greatly differing forcefulness. It is most clearly measured where the standpoint of the narrator at the moment of narration is expressly stated. In the first-person novel this point is often fixed precisely to the hour and minute, as in *Tristram Shandy* and in *Moby-Dick*. The authorial narrator, on the other hand, is usually content with a more or less vague indication of his posteriority to the narrated material. Here again one can recognize the tendency of the authorial narrator to keep his relationship to the narrated material as imprecise as possible in order to give himself free rein. Moreover the authorial narrator in no way feels himself permanently committed to some initially specified temporal distance from the narrated events. Frequently he moves right up to the scene. In this case, of course, the authorial narrative situation is suspended and another mode of mediation, the figural or neutral mode, goes into effect.

The reader's image of the narrative process in an authorial narrative situation depends greatly on various clues in the text which reveal the narrative situation. They adjust the reader's imagination to the perspective and narrative distance of the authorial narrator.

The beginning of the story itself in *Tom Jones* is characteristic of the approximate indication of narrative distance in the typical authorial novel:

> In that part of the western division of this kingdom, which is commonly called Somersetshire, there lately lived (and perhaps, lives still) a gentleman whose name was Allworthy, and who might well be called the favourite of both Nature and Fortune.
>
> (Book I, Chapter 2)

Smollett leaves the narrative distance even less precise:

> In a certain county of England, bounded on one side by the sea, and at the distance of one hundred miles from the metropolis, lived Gamaliel Pickle, Esq., the father of that hero whose adventures we purpose to recall. (*Peregrine Pickle*, Chapter 1)

Even when the precise date of the historical background is indicated, narrative distance cannot always be calculated by comparing the date of the action of the historical background and the date of the genesis of the novel. The author can conceive of himself in relation to the action at a smaller or larger narrative distance than can be established from these two dates. Examples of the latter case can be found in several novels of E. M. Forster, where certain anticipations and prefigurations of the characters' future occasionally reach far beyond the historical date when the novel was written.[9]

At the conclusion of a novel the reader will find some indication of the narrative distance at the point where the time of the action flows into the time level of the act of narration. This opening of the time of action toward the narrative act then brings about a shift of the narrative tense from preterite to present. The fairy tale also makes use of this confluence of the time of action and the present time of the narrator. It is expressed in the

stereotypical ending: "And if they haven't died they're still alive
today."* In *Tom Jones* this final confluence is already anticipated
at the beginning of the narrative, as the passage above shows. At
the end of the novel it again becomes quite clear that the narrator
tells the story of Tom Jones and Sophia Western only a few
years after their happy union:

> [Blifil] lives in one of the northern counties, about 200 miles
> distant from London, and lays up 200£. a year . . . and as to
> Thwackum, he continues at his vicarage . . . Mrs. Fitzpatrick is
> separated from her husband, and retains the little remains of her
> fortune . . . Sophia hath already produced him [Tom] two fine
> children, a boy and a girl, of whom the old gentleman is so fond,
> that he spends much of his time in the nursery, where he declares
> the tattling of his little grand-daughter, who is above a year and a
> half old, is sweeter music than the finest cry of dogs in England.
>
> (Book XVIII, Chapter the Last)

In the same way the time of action flows into the present time
of the narrator at the conclusion of *Joseph Andrews, Barchester
Towers,* and a number of other authorial novels. This type of
conclusion naturally represents a part of the guise of the narrative act; by means of the guise there is generally an attempt to
harmonize the authorial realm and the fictional world.

This flowing of the time of action into the time level of the
narrative act can also be observed in the first-person novel. The
conclusion of *Moll Flanders* is an example. In the narrative situation of the first-person novel, however, this flowing of the time
of action into the narrative time has further significance. It
strengthens the identity of the experiencing and narrating self;
this identity is often presented very loosely in the course of the
narrative.

Deductions concerning the narrative distance also arise from
the use of the two kinds of perspective which Percy Lubbock
calls "scenic" and "panoramic."[10] A narrator may frequently use
a panoramalike survey to bring in past material, to anticipate the

* Cf. the English equivalent: "And they lived happily ever after."—Translator's note.

future, and to recapitulate an event and incorporate it into the pattern of the total action. This technique will continually make the reader aware of the posteriority of the narrator's standpoint vis-à-vis the narrated material. The perspective of the survey, of the broad view in retrospect, also helps form the style of the narrative. The main characteristic of a report from a temporally distant standpoint is the compression of the narrated matter. Compression is simplification, selection, but at the same time, evaluation and interpretation of the fictional world. An individual event is removed from the dense context of intertwining relationships. If necessary it is stripped of the mass of details in which it really appeared; it is placed within clear lines of development, into the perspective of a distant goal.

Writers distinguish themselves by their manner of compression. The author can choose among various technical forms of compression, such as durative, iterative, and punctual compression. His choice will depend on whether emphasis is placed on the duration of an event, on the continual repetition of an event, or on its function as a link in a chain of events in the narrative.[11] It is not possible here to go into the interpretation and meaning which are given to the narrated material by specific kinds of compressive presentation. Horst Oppel's study of the Victorian novel clarifies this function of compression.[12]

Here it is important to understand compression above all as a consequence of the distance of the narrator's standpoint from the narrated action. The reportlike style peculiar to compressive narration directs the reader's imagination away from the narrated material directly back to the narrator. Thus it is possible that even in *Peregrine Pickle,* where the standpoint of the narrator is not directly designated, the reader nevertheless perceives the narrative distance. Smollett employs a highly compressive reportlike style which causes the action to move along at a rapid pace. Wilhelm Dibelius has established that Smollett's work represents a kind of regression in the development of fictional techniques past Fielding and back to Nashe and Defoe. This is explained in large part by Smollett's predominant use of a highly compressive report-like style, while Fielding uses a much more scenic, relaxed technique.[13] With the help of interpolated scenes the course of the action in *Tom Jones* is subjected to a much stronger process of intentional structuring. The thread of the action unwinds with varying speed. While Tom's childhood and youth until his expulsion from Allworthy's house appear in relatively high compression, the months of his wanderings and picaresque adventures are narrated in great detail and with extensive use of scenic presentation, especially in the form of dialogue.[14] Yet the impression of authorial narration is never lost completely, for Fielding can evoke the presence of the authorial narrator again and again in the most varied ways. The narrative elements which call the reader's attention to the act of narration are above all the essayistic excursuses, the interspersed commentary, and finally every epithet which in any sense reflects the author's attitude toward the action.

The determination of the narrator's standpoint and the narrative distance with its effect on the narrative have been given so much attention here because the time and place of the narrative act—the now-and-here of the narrator—are of great significance for the mediation of fictional reality into the reader's imagination. As was already established in the first chapter, the reader in the authorial narrative situation sees the fictional world as if he were looking over the shoulder of the author. Along with the picture of the fictional world the picture of the narrator simultaneously enters the reader's imagination. As a result he uses the now-and-here of the narrator as the basis of his orientation in the fictional world. The reader's center of orientation in the authorial novel therefore lies in the authorial medium. The narrated material appears as past; the epic preterite has the imaginative value of the past. Yet even in clearly authorial novels there are long passages in which the presence of the narrator is not evoked—passages in which the action is presented only slightly compressed and in predominantly scenic form. There are frequently scenes in dialogue with only scattered short comments in the nature of stage directions. The last two-thirds of *Tom Jones* is full of such passages. The question arises thus whether during the reading of these parts the reader's center of orientation remains situated in the now-and-here of the narrator. Even the dialogue in an authorial novel is actually quotation by the narrator. In an oral presentation of such a passage the voice of the narrator would still always remain somehow preceptible behind the expression of individual peculiarities in the characters' speech. Nevertheless, the power to create the effect of presentness in such scenes is often so great that the impression of dramatic-scenic presentation can completely conceal the impression of the authorial report. In this case it will depend mostly on the nature of the individual reader whether and how quickly the original narrative situation is dislodged from the imagination. If this occurs, the reader finds himself on a level with the action, as if he were experiencing it as a witness. His center of orientation no longer lies in the now-and-here of the narrator, but rather in that of an imaginary observer on the scene. As was already noted, the epic preterite in this narrative situation has the imaginative value of the present. The very forms of the epic preterite which occur most frequently in such scenes, the *verba dicendi*, offer but little semantic resistance to a time shift, for they are no longer concretized in the full extent of their meaning. Perhaps one can see an effect of this in the linguistic phenomenon of phonetic reduction, which is more common in the *verba dicendi* than in other verbs; note for example the reduction from *quoth* to *koth, ko, ka*.[15]

It is, however, quite conceivable that a reader, despite long scenic presentation, despite long scenes in dialogue, may not lose sight of the presence of the narrator. For this reader the original authorial narrative situation is retained even in this case. The reader with this type of imagination has probably become quite rare, since in recent times, due to the prevalence of the figural novel, the direct creation of presentness has become the predominating imaginative mode in reading novels. In conclusion it can be said that even in the authorial novel a direct creation of the effect of presentness in the narrated material is temporarily possible. The condition for this is the disappearance of the author for a long stretch of the novel, so that his now-and-here is not evoked and the reader does not become aware of the narrative distance. The authorial novel has this effect above all in dialogue scenes.

The next phenomenon of the authorial narrative situation is the narrator's interpolation of interfering remarks and commentary into the narration of the plot. The relevance to the narrative situation is obvious. Distance gives the narrator the advantage of surveying the action from a position of superiority. Yet the Olympian pose of omniscience here is almost completely taboo. Intrusion and commentary originate mainly from insight into human nature, from a deeper understanding of the action, and from a more mature power of judgment than the characters themselves can possess. Naturally the expression of superior insight and maturity will have to accord with the specific guise of the narrator. Tension then arises between the characters' own interpretation of their experiences, and the authorial narrator's comments and reflections. This tension distinguishes the structure of meaning of the authorial novel from that of other novel forms. It appears again in another form in the first-person novel; the tension occurs between the world of the experiencing self and the world of the narrating self. It remains incomprehensible that the exponents of the normative validity of the "objective" novel could fully overlook this possibility in the structure of the authorial novel. Failure to recognize the peculiar structure of meaning of this novel form can lead to grave critical errors.[16] For this reason it is quite surprising when even studies which attempt to explore the structural forms of the novel ignore this relationship. A. A. Mendilow, for example, wants to ban all authorial commentary:

. . . the merest hint of the author's existence is sufficient to burst the delicate bubble of illusion. It is true that fiction does not, and cannot, and should not if it could, reproduce life photographically;

it must comment on it and interpret it. But the comment must be implicit in the whole; it must flower up from within, not be stitched on from without. A purple patch is still a patch.

(*Time and the Novel*, pp. 101–02).

It cannot be denied that in the novels of Fielding, Thackeray, Trollope, especially Meredith, and a number of other authors numerous comments are to be found which would better have been withheld. The picaresque adventures of Tom Jones, however, could not conceivably have captured the interest of adult readers for two centuries if these readers were not concerned with observing the high intellectual play of the narrator in his attempt to make the rather coarse experiences of Tom Jones literarily presentable. Precisely in *Tom Jones* one can observe that the narrator in such a novel does not make merely autobiographical remarks about an otherwise very simple story, but rather he arouses the reader's interest above all in the narrator as the "one who evaluates, senses, visualizes. He symbolizes the epistemological view held since Kant that we do not apprehend the world as it is in itself, but as it has passed through the medium of an observing mind."[17] In aesthetic terms this important insight could be stated thus: only that world is aesthetically interesting and worthy of presentation which becomes visible through the intellect of a sensitive medium which has humanly interesting traits. The authorial novel realizes this aesthetic perspective mainly through the narrator's peculiar relationship to fictional reality. In the figural novel this perspective presents itself by opening up a consciousness which belongs to a figure of fictional reality. *Tom Jones* is hardly conceivable as a figural novel. None of the figures in the novel could meet the demands which would be made on a figural medium with the task of "dematerializing" the picaresque adventures of Tom Jones. The ideal case of a figural medium which is most subtly attuned to the world it must mirror and which masterfully accomplishes its mediative task is Lambert Strether in *The Ambassadors*; he is treated more thoroughly in a later chapter.

From the large number of authorial comments only that type

will be selected here which seems to stand in direct relationship to the authorial medium's main features—non-membership in the fictional reality, narrative distance, and superior insight. The kind of commentary in question lays claim to general validity. Every artistic creation attempts to present the particular, the unique, the individual in relation to what is general, typical, absolutely valid. In the general comments of the authorial novel this intent is expressed in discursive form. This should actually defeat its own purpose, since the general in art can only be symbolized or implied by the presentation of the particular. This commentary, however, only claims or appears to be "generally valid." Its significance for the structure of meaning of the novel results less from its content than from its effect as a foil; the individual and the particular are set against it. Its importance also results from the fact that it serves especially to emphasize the authorial source of the narration. In this way authorial commentary can play a decisive role in the tension between narrator and fictional reality. The reader is almost always aware that the claim of universal vadidity of this commentary is really an irony.

In Fielding much of what is usually interspersed in the narrative as commentary is gathered together in the essayistic sections. When commentary appears in the narrative it often serves Fielding's intention to make some of his rather rudimentary remarks on the psychology and philosophy of life sound quite self-evident. "I believe it is a true observation, that few secrets are divulged to one person only; but certainly it would be next to a miracle, that a fact of this kind should be known to a whole parish, and not transpire any farther" (Book II, Chapter 5). Criticism of contemporary conditions also appears in this form. In the following example alone the length of the topical commentary indicates that some claim is made to general validity, although there is no attempt to defend or even prove the statement:

> To say the truth, Mr. Allworthy's situation had never been so bad, as the great caution of the doctor had represented: but as a wise general never despises his enemy, however inferior that enemy's force may be, so neither does a wise physician ever de-

spise a distemper, however inconsiderable. As the former preserves the same strict discipline, places the same guards, employs the same scouts, though the enemy be never so weak; so the latter maintains the same gravity of countenance, and shakes his head with the same significant air, let the distemper be never so trifling: and both, among many other good ones, may assign this solid reason for their conduct, that by these means the greater glory redounds to them if they gain the victory, and the less disgrace, if by any unlucky accident they should happen to be conquered.

(Book V, Chapter 8)

As is obvious from the quotation, Fielding did not always fully escape the temptation to inflate the commentary with things which would more properly stand in the narrative section. Commentary with a claim to general validity is most effective in pregnant, short, aphoristic formulations. It usually appears in this form in Jane Austen's novels. In her works, too, the irony of the claim to general validity stands out distinctly because of the rather strong contrast of the commentary with the narrative. Jane Austen was obviously aware that the claim to validity made in the commentary is not always to be taken literally. An almost classical example is to be found in the very first sentence of *Pride and Prejudice:* "It is a truth universally acknowledged, that a single man in possession of a good fortune must be in want of a wife." Andrew H. Wright remarks pertinently: "That this statement is meant to have ironic qualification is shown both in the orotundity of the diction, and by contrast with what is said in the following sentence—that the concern is to be not with the universe but with a 'neighborhood,' not with the totality of mankind, but with 'the surrounding families.' "[18] In this way certain conclusions can be draw from the so-called generally valid commentary and from the degree of its ironic tension with the associated action. These conclusions will provide important clues for the attitude of the authorial narrator toward the narrated material and for his treatment of fictional reality.

We have yet to discuss the manipulation and employment of the technique of point of view in the authorial novel. Just as in the discussion of the modes of narration, opinions are very divergent concerning the question of the choice, definition, and limitation of the narrator's point of view. This is not a complete coincidence, since obvious connections exist between the mode of narration and the technique of point of view. The exponents of predominantly scenic presentation, which is unquestionably the formally stricter mode of narration, have frequently demanded at the same time a strict and consistent fixation of the point of observation and thus also of the perspective and sphere of observation. In the figural novel a change of the point of view from which the fictional world is observed also entails a change of the figural medium. Unity of the figural medium and thus of the point of view throughout the novel represents, in a sense, the ideal case. Percy Lubbock, who must be viewed as the most important theoretical exponent of the strict point-of-view technique, therefore gives very high rank to the later novels of Henry James, where the point of observation is maintained with consistency. He gives special recognition to *The Ambassadors*, in which everything, almost without exception, is seen from the point of view of a single figural medium.[19]

In the authorial novel such a strict use of point of view can hardly be justified. Numerous authors make extensive use in their authorial novels of the ability freely to change the point of view and to relocate the perspective and the sphere of observation. Perhaps they are even a bit too carefree at times and earn for themselves in this way the criticism of the opposition, which advocates strict respect for one point of view. With insight and moderation E. M. Forster practiced and championed in his novels and his book on the novel the practice of free point-of-view technique. In *Aspects of the Novel* he explicitly protests Lubbock's overestimation*—as he sees it—of the consistent point-of-view technique. "For me the 'whole intricate question of method' resolves itself not into formulae but into the power of the writer to bounce the reader into accepting what he says. . . ."[20] For this purpose the author should naturally be permitted to alter his

* Forster's book appeared in 1927; Lubbock's *The Craft of Fiction* was first published in 1921.—Translator's note.

point of view as well as his realm of observation and his degree of familiarity with his characters' thoughts. As long as an author employs this free point-of-view technique with the prudent moderation of E. M. Forster, the technique needs no further justification. The restriction of the point of view and the establishment of a perspective will always be grounded in the narrative situation and in the specific guise of the authorial narrator. These conventions may satisfy the reader's illusion expectancy without requiring consistent use of a point-of-view technique. *Tom Jones* again serves as an example. In this novel the narrator presents himself as a chronicler who endeavors to acquaint himself fully with the life of his hero. Although the narrator never gives any indication that the hero himself even once served as his informant, there is no lack of detailed presentation of the hero's thoughts and feelings, which the narrator could never have learned except from the mouth of the hero himself. The reader who directs his interest more toward the narrated material than the narrative process is generally not disturbed by this contradiction between the narrator's guise and his point of view. This contradiction is also largely concealed by frequent assertions by the narrator that he was unable, despite all efforts, to obtain reliable information about this or that. The narrator occasionally pretends to resort to his own speculations in some matter:

> I have thought it somewhat strange, upon reflection, that the housekeeper never acquainted Mrs. Blifil with this news, as women are more inclined to communicate all pieces of intelligence to their own sex, than to ours. The only way, as it appears to me, of solving this difficulty, is, by imputing it to that distance which was now grown between the lady and the housekeeper. . . .
>
> (Book II, Chapter 5)

Despite its various guises the authorial medium retains some of the authorial free rein, by which means it appears as the mask and manifestation of the author-creator of the narrative. The indistinctness of its mode of existence also serves, as the mask of the author, to refer to the real world while at the same time, on the basis of its guise as a chronicler of the action, referring to the fictional world of the figures. Because of its continuous self-characterization and bodily presence as a figure of the fictional world, a figural medium is as a rule more sharply profiled than an authorial medium. In addition, the characteristic traits of an authorial medium are not simply those of the author who hides behind them. For this reason alone they are difficult to grasp. The author only rarely puts his entire personality into the manifestation of the authorial medium. It is usually only a partial self-portrait in which often very striking traits of the author are absent or to which new traits are added. Frequently a rearrangement can be observed in the value system as an author projects himself into his authorial medium, so that the picture of the authorial medium differs from that of the author in important points. In short, the concept of the authorial medium serves not only to designate the point of view and source of narration. It serves above all to call attention to the nature and change of the author's physiognomy or personality and to the idiosyncracy of his consciousness. In this way the authorial medium can be distinguished from the personality of the real author.

The reader, due to his illusion expectancy, views the events of the plot as primary and its narration as secondary and posterior. For purposes of analysing the process of presentation this order can be reversed. The action of the fable then presents itself as the result of the process of conception and the act of narration. One can regard the reader's illusion expectancy in an authorial novel and the corresponding conventions as the fiction of reversing the true relationship. The reportlike mode of narration and for that matter the whole convention of authorial narration support this fiction. What originated with the author, with his flash of inspiration, and with his fantasy—all this reappears in the guise of the narrator, *sub specie auctoris*. This insight can be important in modern novels for the interpretation of certain passages where a kind of shifting narrative situation predominates. In the authorial novel the mediative function can occasionally be turned over to a figural medium for some part of the presentation. The material presented through such a figural medium is not always stripped of all traces of its originally authorial provenance. In general the reader does not even become aware of this ambivalence. For the theory of literature these traces of authorial provenance in material presented figurally reveal a good deal. They serve to illuminate the creative process. Traces of authorial provenance can be detected, for example, in Virginia Woolf's novel *Mrs. Dalloway*, which is predominantly figural.[21] In this novel the author's characteristic mode of seeing and experiencing things shines through a figure's mode of experiencing. This occurs whenever that figure takes over the mediative function and thus acts as a figural medium.

The transfer of authorial views to a figural medium can be followed more clearly in the analysis of an image which appears in Hightower's death scene in William Faulkner's *Light in August*. Hightower lives the last hour of his life sitting at the window of his house, looking out. Outside a summer day comes to a sultry, colorful close. Hightower's life passes once more before his eyes, and as it becomes darker his thoughts progress more and more slowly from scene to scene. In order to describe this gradual failure of the life functions and the approaching decline of thought into empty, automatic, rotation the narrator introduces the image of a wheel sinking into the sand. The rotation of the wheel becomes slower and slower, so that it can only just propel the vehicle forward and finally brings it to a halt. "Thinking begins to slow now. It slows like a wheel beginning to run in sand, the axle, the vehicle, the power which propels it not yet aware" (*Light in August*, p. 462). This image is expanded in later passages. It continues to be used by the narrator to describe the gradual diminishing of the dying man's energies. But then the image of the wheel suddenly appears in a vision of the dying man himself. The narrator's image of the wheel spinning in the sand emerges in Hightower's own consciousness surrounded by a halo in which the faces of the dying man's acquaintances appear:

> The wheel, released, seems to rush on with a long sighing sound. He sits motionless in its aftermath, in his cooling sweat,

while the sweat pours and pours. The wheel whirls on. It is going
fast and smooth now, because it is freed now of burden, of vehicle,
axle, all. In the lambent suspension of August into which night is
about to fully come, it seems to engender and surround itself with
a faint glow like a halo. The halo is full of faces. . . .   (p. 465)

The context shows that the first passage and to all appearances
the beginning of the second passage belong to the narration of
an authorial narrator. The end of the second passage, however,
must be viewed as the direct rendering of Hightower's consciousness. The image and the idea of the wheel have slipped out
of the authorial realm into a figural realm. Two pages after the
first introduction of the wheel by the narrator one reads: "Thinking is running too heavily now; he should know it, sense it. Still
the vehicle is unaware of what it is approaching. 'And after all, I
have paid. I have bought my ghost . . .' " (p. 464). The first two
sentences are distinctly spoken by the narrator. It cannot be a
case of the rendering of a figural consciousness. This is clear from
the following sentence in which the contents of Hightower's
consciousness are presented in the form of an interior monologue
supplemented by quotation marks to indicate the direct rendering
of consciousness. In this way the direct rendering of consciousness
is set off clearly from the authorial narration. There are as yet no
indications that the image of the wheel is in some way anticipated
in Hightower's consciousness. Only in the above passage beginning with "the wheel, released . . ." does the image of the wheel
gradually dissociate itself from the authorial realm and become
the basic motif of Hightower's dying vision. It is also remarkable
that this shifting of the image is accompanied by a certain
ambiguity in the syntax. The image of the wheel is evoked for
the first time in the distinctly figural realm with a pronoun ("it
seems to engender"). This signifies that the image must have
already emerged in Hightower's consciousness. Yet the narrative
provides no clear evidence of this. Moreover, between this
pronoun and its antecedent, "wheel," in "the wheel whirls on"
there comes a whole series of concepts and ideas. Some readers
will perhaps not even make the proper connection.

To pursue this question further does not seem worthwhile. On the one hand, Faulkner's style would not stand the test, since it proves to be imprecise and more rhetorically than logically consistant. On the other hand the line would quickly be passed which bounds the region where the structure of meaning is still recognizable for the reader. To go beyond this region would not serve the theory of the novel.

It seems to lie in the nature of the literary creative process that certain authorial elements constantly make their way into the fictional world and into the consciousness of its figures. Such elements—series of ideas, image complexes, and associations—actually belong to the consciousness of the authorial medium, that is, to the self-created personal manifestation of the author. Naturally everything in a narrative originates with the author. In the course of objectifying and dramatizing the fictional figures, however, the author must always endeavor to break off these initial ties, to conceal them from the eyes of the reader. In general this will take place by suppressing the association, the image, or the idea in one of the realms, either the authorial or the figural. Another possibility for such dissimilation consists of developing the whole association to such an extent in the figural realm that its origin in an idea from the authorial realm is no longer immediately recognizable. Any true objectification amounts basically to this process of dissimilating the authorial idea.

A reversal of this shifting of an originally authorial element into the consciousness of a figural medium occurs in the "contamination" of the author's language by the language of a fictional figure. The term "contamination" was applied by Leo Spitzer to a process observed in the travel sketches of Alfred Kerr.[22] In the narrative report of the authorial medium linguistic peculiarities appear which were first noted in the speech of the figures portrayed. Both phenomena are basically a result of the same process. The consciousness of the author gives rise to all of fictional reality. The process of objectification, however, is sometimes not fully accomplished, so that "contamination" of this sort may occur between the authorial and the figural realms.

III

THE FIRST-PERSON NOVEL

IN MOST THEORETICAL TREATMENTS of the novel the first-person novel is considered a unified form clearly distinct from the third-person form. This seems to be the real reason why no attempt has been made to view the first-person novel as one typical form in the endless number of formative possibilities which the novel offers in a continuous, ever-changing series. This continuous development of the novel in forms and types is immediately evident when the novel is viewed by taking the narrative situation as its most important structural feature.

It has already been shown that in the typical authorial novel the separation of the authorial realm from the fictional world can be suspended by the guise of the narrative process. Nevertheless, the author hesitates in general to establish personal relations between the authorial narrator and his figures. While such relations are never directly stated in *Tom Jones*, the authorial narrator in *Joseph Andrews* tells the reader that at least one figure of the novel personally confided to him a large part of the story. This sort of link can be extended to so many figures of a novel that the authorial narrator ultimately appears himself as a figure in the fictional world. When the authorial narrator is drawn into the world of the characters in this way, attributes of the characters' mode of existence are transferred to him in the imagination of the reader. The authorial narrator becomes a first-person narrator, for according to the extent to which he makes his way into the figural realm, he seems to lose the authorial narrator's characteristic reluctance to refer to himself in the first-person singular. This transformation of the authorial narrator into a first-person narrator is a first breach in the apparently impenetrable wall separating the third-person novel and the first-person novel. One begins to see the way in which the first-person novel will be linked to the authorial novel in the continuous chain of novel forms.

The identity of the realms of existence of the narrator and the fictional world forms the foundation of the narrative situation in the first-person novel. In the authorial novel this potential identity was only superficially suggested in the narrative guise and only occasionally realized in isolated ties of the narrator to a figure. The first-person narrator distinguishes himself from the novel's other characters only by his desire for expression and presentation. Their world is his world and their fate is not infrequently his, too.

Before describing the typical forms of the first-person novel it is necessary to show how a borderline position can be realized between the typical kinds of authorial novel on the one hand and the typical forms of the first-person novel on the other. In *The History of Henry Esmond Written by Himself* Thackeray's narrative situation straddles the fence between the authorial novel and the first-person novel. The narrator plays the authorial role as long as he reports the story of his hero—which is also his own story—in the third person. Just as in part of the title, the narrator again and again reveals his identity with the hero; in a few places he even narrates in the first person.

In the typical first-person novel the illusion of the identity of the narrator and a figure from the fictional world is continually renewed by the use of the pronoun "I." The resulting structural uniqueness of the first-person novel will be treated further in the interpretation of *Moby-Dick* below. At this point, however, it is necessary to summarize the peculiar double appearance of the "I" in the novel. This "I" or "self" reveals itself to the reader as a figure experiencing the events of the plot—a figure which ultimately becomes the narrator of those events. As a rule the experiencing process is separated from the narrating process by a more or less clearly marked time span which corresponds to the narrative distance of the authorial novel. In the future a distinction will thus be made between the *experiencing self* and the *narrating self*. The prostitute, the thief, "the gentlewoman" Moll Flanders is the experiencing self; the Moll Flanders who narrates her adventurous past with that peculiar mixture of repentance and retrospective gusto is the narrating self in Defoe's novel. Henry Esmond's relationship, as a narrator of his own life, to Henry Esmond, the hero of the memoires, is incomparably more subtle. Thackeray varies greatly the illumination in which the identity of narrator and hero appears. Although the reader never fully loses sight of the announced autobiographical guise of the narrative, the narrator's predominant third-person reference to his hero can bring about an imaginative mode which really corresponds to the authorial narrative situation. Under these circumstances special significance accrues to the passages of the novel which are narrated in the first person.

The first-person plural is used several times in the sense of a collective reference to Henry Esmond and his comrades either in the army or in prison. But in addition there are two particularly striking moments where the first-person singular is used. Both passages narrate experiences of the hero which are accompanied by violent emotions. The first passage occurs at the end of the thirteenth chapter of the second book; it describes Henry Esmond's visit to the grave of his mother, whom he never knew. The second passage is in the seventh chapter of the third book; Henry Esmond meets Rachel Castlewood again after a long separation. She is now mistress of the family estate of his own paternal ancestors; it is she whom he will ultimately marry. The strong pressure of images from the past causes the narrator to discard the authorial distance of the third-person reference and to continue the narrative in the first person. For many a reader this change in the reference from third person to first person will pass unnoticed. Yet the reader probably cannot escape the effect which comes from suspending the narrator's authorial distance by means of the direct identification of the narrator with the experiencing figure. At the same time the reverse process must be noted in this novel. The narrator takes pleasure in occasionally objectifying himself, as it were, as a figure by referring to himself in the act of narration in the third-person singular.[1]

For this study the description of the narrative situation of *Henry Esmond* serves to prove that it is possible to realize intermediary forms which unite characteristic aspects of the surrounding novel types—and that such intermediary forms can actually be encountered among the great narrative works of literature. Although such novels assume borderline positions between the typical forms, the narrative situation in no way impairs the reader's imagination. Thus the narrator is capable of occupying every point on the road from the authorial novel to the first-person novel. In the authorial narrative situation the narrator's characteristic relationship to the figures of the novel corresponds to the manifold relationships between the narrating self and the experiencing self in the first-person narrative situation. Between these two typical narrative situations a novel theorist can pinpoint innumerable intermediary forms through which the narrative situation moves in continuous succession from one type to the other. This does not always necessitate a change in reference from third person to first person. The authorial narrative situation can closely approximate the first-person situation by penetrating further and further into the fictional world, while retaining the third-person form of reference. Conversely, the narrative situation of the first-person novel can approach the authorial narrative situation by shifting the presentational center of gravity from the experiencing self to the narrating self. Here another character usually occupies the center of the action, while the first-person narrator withdraws as a relatively uninvolved witness to the outskirts of the action. Such variations of the typical narrative situation are very common.

Just to show that even the change of reference in *Henry*

Esmond is not a unique instance, a similar case in a more recent novel can be noted. Robert Penn Warren's *All the King's Men* (1946) is a first-person novel in which the narration switches several times to the third person. This transition is not always made as smoothly and inconspicuously as in *Henry Esmond*. In Warren's novel the first-person narrator, whose name is Jack Burden, is not himself the main figure in the action. Although he in fact plays the real lead in the moral and intellectual action, he appears in the surface action as the henchman of his boss, Willie Stark. The first-person narrator's eccentric position is the reason why long stretches of the novel contain no real first-person references. Much is narrated about the central figure of the action and a number of other figures; there are, however, comparatively few passages when the first-person narrator has occasion to include his own experiencing self in this history. From a given page of such a section it is often impossible to decide whether the work is a first-person novel or a third-person novel. The personal traits of the first-person narrator fade before the vivid portraits of the other figures. This, too, can be viewed as an element of authorial narration. In the fourth chapter of the novel the first-person narrator's counterpart in the fictional world, the experiencing self, is presented in the third person. The experiencing self is called simply Jack Burden; except for the beginning and concluding paragraphs of this chapter, however, there is no direct reference—by a pronoun, for example—to the narrating self. The reason for this change of reference is completely different from the one in *Henry Esmond*. The author wishes to add a new figure, Cass Mastern, to his gallery of characters. This is done by having the narrator cite long passages directly from Cass's first-person journal. The author was evidently faced with the problem of avoiding any confusion which might arise between the two first-person narrators while at the same time preserving the sense of immediacy in the content of the journal. His solution was to transform the original "I" of the main narrator into an objectified third-person novel figure and retain the first-person narrative situation of the journal. Simple reduplications of the original narrative situation are not uncommon. The first-person narrative situation in Emily Brontë's *Wuthering Heights* is trebled in some chapters. *All the King's Men* represents a special case of such reduplication of the narrative situation, for it contains a simultaneous change from the first-person reference to the third person. Warren seems not to give his readers full credit for being able to comprehend completely the resulting concentric pattern or to follow easily the transformation of the first-person figure into a third-person. Perhaps for this reason the transitional signals are very explicit: "This Jack Burden (of whom the present Jack Burden, *Me*, is a legal, biological, and perhaps even metaphysical continuator) lived in a slatternly apartment . . ." (p.280, cf. also p. 249). The hasty reader will doubtless be thankful for such clues. At the same time they focus the reader's attention very sharply on the manipulations which are necessary if the narrator is to accomplish his purpose. In the narrative situation of a first-person novel where the act of narration is clearly marked such manipulations are by no means rare; sometimes the narrator alludes to them explicitly. In addition the narrating self retains certain traits which recall his relationship to an authorial narrator. One of these authorial traits is his ability to put, if necessary, the same kind of distance between himself and the experiencing self as usually prevails between an authorial narrator and his figures.

If all first-person novels were arranged in a continuous spectrum of novel forms according to degree of presentation of the narrative act, they would readily distribute themselves in two different directions. To one side we would find those first-person novels in which the narrative process itself undergoes more or less thorough presentation. To the other side we would see those first-person novels in which the act of narration receives no explicit mention in the text or where the consciousness of the narrating self is so unobtrusive that one cannot really speak of "narrating." The group which incorporates the narrative process departs from the first-person novel's typical narrative situation in the direction of the authorial novel. The group which does not present the act of narration moves off from the pole of the first-person novel in the direction of the figural novel. For a typology of the novel certain conclusions can be drawn from this observation; these will be presented at the end of this study.

No matter whether the first-person narrator plays a central or a peripheral role in the action; whether he actively or passively participates as the main figure; or whether he is a secondary figure, an observing, registering witness and commentator of the action —in every case two strands of experience are always united in his person as long as the narrative act is incorporated into the presentation. As a central figure in the action or even as a simple participant he belongs to a world of deeds, adventures, tension, and crises. Experiences of this nature are usually assigned to the younger period of the narrator, the experiencing self. The corresponding time is always presented as a single span of time, although the size of the segment from the hero's life and the degree of compression of the narrative can vary greatly. But as soon as the act of narration is sufficiently characterized the same figure—now as the narrating self—generally takes on an entirely different shape. Cut off from its earlier experiences, the narrating self yields completely to retrospective reflection. The time of crises and tempests is now past. The time corresponding to the narrating self can also become a visible time span; this is the case in *Tristram Shandy,* for example. More often, however, the extent of this time is not precisely designated. Perhaps only one point, one moment of the time may be fixed by a date, as will be seen in *Moby-Dick.* Sometimes the whole characterization of this time span is limited to the simple indication of its posteriority to the time period of the experiencing self; this is already inherent in the narrative situation itself (someone narrates his own experiences). In *Roderick Random* the time of the narrative act is left indefinite in this manner.

In the narrative situation of the first-person novel the temporal distance from the narrative act to the experiences of the experiencing self constitutes the distance to the narrated material. Insofar as this interval of narrative distance is designated it forms an important element in the structure of the first-person novel. The narrative distance is the measure, as it were, of the interval between narrating and experiencing self. As such it indicates the degree of alienation and tension between these two manifestations of the self. In changing from actor to author the self undergoes a development, a maturing process, a change of interest, which often comes to the fore in the novel. In interpreting a work it is therefore useful to proceed from the determination of the narrative distance; we can fix the mental perspective in which the time of the experiencing self is observed from the point of view of the older, more mature, self-possessed, narrating self. This makes it easier to comprehend the interpretation of the action which is inherent in the process of narration. This indicates the road which will be taken by the following interpretation of *Moby-Dick*. The possibility of such an approach naturally depends on the extent to which the narrating self is characterized in the novel. Like the presence of the authorial narrator in the third-person novel, the presence of the narrating self in the narrative act of the first-person novel can reveal itself to varying degrees. The adult Tristram Shandy as first-person narrator steps up to the reader in his full physical presence at the moment of composition. He even allows the reader glimpses into the ostensibly random course of the story's conception. In this novel the now-and-here of the narrating self is precisely fixed in place and time, so that ultimately the narrative process becomes the real action. In this case the narrative act also constitutes the only chain of action which is presented with chronological consistency. All the other groups of episodes are merely linked to the narrative process by association.[2] In this respect *Tristram Shandy* represents an extreme case in which the narrative act has overrun the actual narrative. Action at the level of the narrative process as well as the now-and-here of the narrating self are usually portrayed with less emphasis.

The epistolary novel can be viewed as an extension of the first-person novel. The writing of letters is equivalent to the situation of the narrative act. The narrative distance here is sharply curtailed. The action is not reported from a single point but in episodes which are presented immediately after their conclusion or even while they are still taking place.

In a large number of first-person novels the narrative process is indicated either indirectly or not at all. In such a case it is naturally impossible to distinguish the narrating self from the experiencing self. Occasionally the existence of a narrating self can be inferred from references to the past and future. His precise now-and-here, however, remains otherwise uncertain; the narrating self is not evoked in the reader's imagination. Examples of such novels are *Roderick Random* and Melville's early novel *Typee*. Here, too, it will depend on one's reading habits whether an image of the narrative act arises from the very fact of the novel's existence. As has already been established, the predominance of reportlike narration can itself suffice to call attention to the presence of a personal narrator. Predominantly scenic presentation, on the other hand, concentrates the reader's interest on the action and thus on the experiencing self. Thomas Nashe in *The Unfortunate Traveller* and Daniel Defoe in *Moll Flanders* employ for the most part a reportlike mode of narration. In this way the reader is constantly reminded of the existence of a narrating self even though the narrative act remains rather vaguely defined.

In *David Copperfield* Charles Dickens unfolds long stretches of his first-person novel in predominantly scenic presentation. This mode of narration draws the attention of the reader to the experiencing self. If in a first-person novel the scenic presentation is executed to an exclusive and extreme degree, all references to and traces of the narrative act of the narrating self will be eliminated. The self will then appear solely as the experiencing self. The action in such a first-person narrative will consist for the most part of dialogue and the associated processes of consciousness in the self. It may even consist solely of a rendering of the stream of consciousness in the form of an interior monologue. No one "narrates" any longer; the action is "rendered" with no visible narrative mediation, as if it were occurring originally in this state. Thus an important structural feature links this kind of first-person novel to the figural novel, which is also characterized by scenic presentation, withdrawal of the narrating medium, and the predominant presentation of dialogue and processes of consciousness. This kind of first-person novel is seldom realized in long narrative works. Its most consistent use is Molly Bloom's monologue at the end of Joyce's *Ulysses*. The first three chapters of Faulkner's *The Sound and the Fury* also belong to this category. In German literature Arthur Schnitzler is known for his use of this form in his stories *Leutnant Gustl, Die griechische Tänzerin,* and *Fräulein Else*. In all of these works the dialogue which occurs is supplemented only by the monologue of the main figure; in the final chapter of *Ulysses* nothing is presented but Molly's interior monologue.

Another structural peculiarity which this kind of first-person narrative shares with the figural novel is the limited amount of narrated time. By the same token this narrated time is almost always presented without interruption. In Schnitzler's *Leutnant Gustl* the action lasts but a few hours. At one point the presentation skips approximately three hours, during which time the hero is sleeping. The duration of the action in the final chapter of *Ulysses* amounts to less than an hour. The first three chapters of *The Sound and the Fury* each span only a few hours of one day.

The conclusion of each of these works also has a distinctive structure. In *Fräulein Else* the presentation ends as the dying heroine's consciousness is extinguished. Molly Bloom's monologue ends when she is overcome by sleep. Quentin Compson's chapter in *The Sound and the Fury* comes to a close with Quentin's suicide. Such "self-activating" conclusions, which make the interference of the narrator superfluous, are characteristic of the figural narrative situation in general.

In summary the theoretical place of the first-person novel can be defined in the following manner. In one form—when the narrative process is clearly emphasized and when the narrating and experiencing selves are separated by a recognizable narrative distance—the first-person novel approaches the narrative situation of the authorial novel. In the other form—when the narrative process, narrative distance, and narrating self are not portrayed in the text—the first-person novel approaches the narrative situation of the figural novel.

This discussion of the first-person novel must be concluded with a brief treatment of the kinds of orientation which can be observed in various first-person forms. The authorial novel, it was established, can shift its center of orientation from the now-and-here of the narrating author to the now-and-here of a figure or an imaginary observer on the scene. When it most closely approaches the narrative situation of the authorial novel the first-person novel (with designated narrative process) contains a similar kind of orientation. The reader's initial center of orientation lies in the now-and-here of the narrating self. From this point the narrated material must appear as past. Then it becomes possible for the reader to direct his attention away from the narrative act and toward the fictional scene. In this way, just as in the authorial novel, the original narrative situation can be suspended in the reader's imagination. The reader then identifies with the experiencing self at the moment of its experience. This shift in the center of orientation most frequently takes place in the authorial novel when scenic presentation prevails over long stretches of the narrative. The shift of the center of orientation in the first-person novel is facilitated by the fact that the narrating self and the experiencing self are only different aspects of the same personality. The shift from the now-and-here of the narrating self to the now-and-here of the experiencing self can thus take place within the same person. Recollection of the past, which is usually the starting point of the narrative process in the first-person novel, will advance all the more easily to a vividly "present" portrayal of the self's earlier experiences.

If the now-and-here of the narrating self is not evoked, which will be the case in the first-person novel with no designation of the narrative act, the reportlike, compressive mode of narration will be replaced by a more detailed, more scenic presentation. Here the reader's center of orientation will be located in the scene or in the experiencing self. Thus this kind of first-person novel anticipates the orientation of the figural novel, where the reader always finds his center of orientation in the now-and-here of a novel figure or of an imaginary observer on the scene. In such a narrative situation the epic preterite will possess a present-time imaginative value; the narrated material will give the illusion of presentness.

Moby-Dick

Herman Melville's *Moby-Dick or, The Whale* (1851) is a first-person novel with an expressly designated act of narration. It is a multileveled, multifaceted work which makes use of almost all the formal possibilities of this novel form. It is first necessary to determine the illusion expectancy which the reader derives from the narrative situation of *Moby-Dick*. At the same time it will be seen whether the author literally fulfills the reader's expectations, whether he ignores them, or whether he attempts to satisfy them with the help of certain narrative conventions. Point for point the following factors—all aspects of the reader's illusion expectancy in this novel—will be examined for their employment and realization in the novel:

1. The narrating self is identical *in persona* with the experiencing self;

2. the narrating self in the act of narration stands in a relationship of posteriority to the experiencing self and to the action; the narrative distance is designated in the narrative;

3. if the narrative distance is greater than the duration of the narrated matter, then the narrating self regards the action as completed; the narrating self then has the privilege of foreknowing all the action to be narrated; for this reason the narrating self can rise to panoramalike surveys; he can give glimpses of partial resolutions or reveal the ending;

4. the narrating self distinguishes itself from the experiencing self by greater insight and maturity, by a tendency to retrospection and reflection, and often by a completely different way of

life; between the experiencing self's experience of an event and the narrative re-creation of the same event at the hands of the narrating self there are therefore differences of valuation and interpretation which become visible in the structure of meaning of the novel.

It should not be necessary to expound in detail the fact that these are not demands which ought to be realized by every first-person novel. These four points simply indicate interpretative aspects useful for investigating the peculiar structure of a first-person novel. Although these factors are all formulated more or less clearly in the reader's illusion expectancy for this kind of novel, previous interpretations have paid almost no attention to them:

Point 1:

Significantly, the novel begins with an explicit *in-persona* identification of the narrating self with the experiencing self, who appears in the narrative as Ishmael:

> Call me Ishmael. Some years ago—never mind how long precisely
> —having little or no money in my purse, and nothing particular
> to interest me on shore, I thought I would sail about a little and
> see the watery part of the world. It is a way I have of driving
> off the spleen. . . .   (Chapter I, p. 1)[3]

With these opening sentences the "he" of the figure Ishmael has already been taken into the "I" self of the narrator. The very opposite process takes place in *Henry Esmond*, where the announcement of the novel as an autobiography made one expect an "I"; the author, however, converted the "I" into a "he."

In *Moby-Dick* the first-person form serves to narrate Ishmael's experiences on the memorable last voyage of the whaler Pequod. In general Ishmael, the experiencing self, bears the point of view from which the events are seen. This definition of the point of observation can hardly be seen as a great restriction of the narrator's scope considering the limited stage of action on a whaling ship of that time. Nevertheless, the narration transcends at several points the borders of this realm of observation. The point of view is respected most strictly in the chapters with a predominant reportlike mode of narration, such as those at the beginning of the novel. Even in the more detailed scenes in which dramatic events of the voyage are presented Ishmael's point of view is in general retained. A narrative convention of the authorial novel appears again here. The narrator, who stands at a great temporal distance, is permitted to reproduce long dialogues as direct quotations although such a feat of memory is beyond what is humanly possible. Since scenic presentation prevails in such passages, the reader's center of orientation lies in the scene; the presence of a narrating self can be ignored temporarily, so that even the logical impossibility of such a detailed reproduction of the distant past is not disturbing.

On several occasions, however, the narrative completely departs from Ishmael's point of view. The reader learns things of which Ishmael could have no knowledge, even after the event. Such chapters are sometimes announced by titles in the style of stage directions in the drama. Chapter XXXVII is entitled "The Cabin; by the stern windows; Ahab sitting alone and gazing out." There follows a presentation of the thoughts of Ahab, who is sitting alone and unobserved in his cabin; this is rendered in the form of an interior monologue or soliloquy. In the same way the following chapters present the sololoquies of the officers Starbuck and Stubb. Nor is Ishmael's presence discernible in the following scene in the forecastle of the ship where the sailors and harpooners are introduced in the manner of a play (XL). In such scenes the narrative self seems to have cast off this identity with the experiencing self; he seems to appear in the role of an unhampered third-person narrator. (This loose, suspensible identity between the first-person narrator and Ishmael will also be revealed in another context.) Yet at the same time attention is constantly called to the *in-persona* identity of the two. Directly following the dramalike cavalcade of sailors one reads: "I, Ishmael, was one of that crew, my shouts had gone up with the rest" (XLI, p. 175). In this context it is also striking that in the first chapters Ishmael's physical presence on board the Pequod is described in great detail; later, however, he seems more and more to lead a peculiar, incorporeal, indefinite existence on board the whaler. To be sure, he returns again and again from this ghost-like existence to his original, fully corporeal mode of appearance, as in the chapter "The Mat-Maker" (XLVII) and the second half of "The Try-Works" (XCVI). Under strikingly similar circumstances the first-person narrator in Conrad's *The Nigger of the Narcissus* also casts aside his corporality and thus temporarily surrenders his established spatio-temporal qualities. This results in a situation not without narrative effectiveness. The reader believes himself in touch with the experiencing self via the narrating self, but he is unable to discern from the collective "we" of the narrative the actual location of the experiencing self somewhere in the crew on deck or in the ropes. In Melville's earlier novel *Omoo* the first-person narrator in very similar circumstances never casts aside his corporality as the experiencing self. This transformation of Ishmael's mode of appearance first appears clearly in Chapter XXIX. The fact that it cannot be observed in earlier chapters makes it probable that this "dematerialization" of the experiencing self is directly connected with the crucial reconception and reworking of the novel. This process has been demonstrated in detail by George R. Stewart.[4] According to Stewart the novel was thoroughly rewritten from Chapter XXIII on, while until this chapter only a few traces of rewriting can be found. This means that only in the rewritten part of the novel does Ishmael acquire the ability to surrender his corporality whenever this seems desirable to the narrator. One could also say that only in the new version of the novel does the narrator transcend the limits of the point of view and occasionally forget about his—Ishmael's—bodily coexistence with the crew of the Pequod. According to all appearances the grand conception of the novel with its permeating metaphysical symbolism was ultimately realized only by means of this reworking. This change in the first-person narrator can thus be explained as a narrative necessity which grew out of the transformation of Melville's "first Moby-Dick," which was conceived in the manner of earlier seafaring novels, to the *Moby-Dick* of world literature.

Several other deviations from the common point-of-view technique can be noted in this first-person novel. A special kind of point of view resulted whenever the individual boats on the chase had to be described. Ishmael supposedly belongs to the crew of Starbuck's boat. One would expect that the center of observation would lie in Starbuck's boat. But the narrator does not always adhere to this perspective. In the chapters "The First Lowering" (XLVIII) and "Stubb Kills a Whale" (LXI) the center of observation clearly lies for a long time in Stubb's boat, not in Starbuck's boat, where the reader assumes Ishmael to be. Of course, Ishmael can have later learned from Stubb's crew what took place there. In that case the narrator has made use of his right to narrate even those events which he has not himself observed, just as if he had witnessed them. Strangely enough, there are no indications of such conversations among the members of the crew. Below decks the crew is treated only as a collective group; the presentation seldom follows them there. The main scene of the narrative lies on the upper deck and in the whaleboats of the Pequod.

The final chapter also departs from the point of view of the first-person narrator. It reports the final day of the hunt for Moby Dick and the ultimate end of the Pequod. Ishmael is now in the boat of Ahab, the captain, who is himself participating in the hunt for the white whale. In this way Ishmael is almost always on the scene of the dramatic action, for Ahab is the most relentless of the hunters. Soon, however, the center of observation begins to dissociate itself from Ishmael. The end of the Pequod, which draws all living creatures with it into the depths, is then reported in a panoramic view. The narrator's point of view is no longer tied to the Pequod or one of its boats; it hovers over the scene of the sinking. The catastrophe can be reported with the epic distance and calm of a nonparticipant: "Now small fowls flew screaming over the yet yawning gulf; a sullen white surf beat against its steep sides; then all collapsed, and the great shroud of the sea rolled on as it rolled five thousand years ago" (CXXXV, p. 566). The cosmic peace which spreads over the scene only moments after the sinking of the Pequod comes as an awesome epilogue; *sub specie aeternitatis,* as it were, it draws the consequences of Ahab's monomaniacal struggle with the incomprehensible, the overwhelming: ". . . and the great shroud of the sea rolled on as it rolled five thousand years ago." Such a conclusion demands the narrative stance of the Olympian observer; it can normally be realized only in the authorial novel with an authorial narrator. The suppression of Ishmael's full corporeal appearance beginning approximately in Chapter XXXIX prepares for the transition to the narrative stance in the final chapter.

The reader, however, will remember Ishmael's detailed self-presentation in the initial chapters. Once established, the narrative situation can no longer be abolished completely from the reader's imagination. Melville, too, must have sensed this, for he added an epilogue which was meant to eliminate the apparent contradiction in the point-of-view technique. In view of the concluding atmosphere of the novel the anticlimactic realism of this epilogue would better have been avoided. Aside from the point-of-view technique, on the other hand, it reestablishes the unity of the novel. It brings the narrative back to the concrete, realistic conception of the beginning. In this context it is significant that the epilogue was absent in the English first edition, which appeared approximately a month before the American first edition.[5] The London edition, however, was set from the pages of the American first edition, for which Melville himself had read the proofs.[6] Vincent and Mansfield think it unlikely that Melville composed the epilogue for the American edition on the objections of English critics who accused the author of lack of consistency in his point-of-view technique. The time between the two editions (London, October 18, 1851, and New York, November 14, 1851) would have been too short.[7] The genesis of the epilogue therefore deserves a more careful examination. Shortly before the end of the novel it is reported that the whale throws three men from Ahab's boat, of whom one drops astern and can no longer be picked up. Attention should be focused on whether this passage was interpolated simultaneously with the addition of the epilogue. The story in the epilogue to the effect that Ishmael was this third man appears on the surface to be little more than a saving flash of inspiration. In this way the narrative dilemma of the conclusion could be solved and the irreplaceable life of the first-person narrator saved. If such a conclusion had been planned and prepared for by the narrator, a bit more attention doubtless would have had to be paid to the first-person narrator as he fell overboard. As it stands he is alloted the laconic sentence: ". . . the third man helplessly dropping astern, but still afloat and swimming" (CXXXV, p. 563).

In conclusion it can be said that the initial close connection between the narrating self and the experiencing self is considerably relaxed throughout most of the work. The narrating self is at times independent of Ishmael, his primary source. At least twice the narrating self is even dissociated from him completely. Like an authorial narrator the narrating self is equipped with an Olympian knowledge which can dispense with all further sources and all ties to a particular point of view. The change in the treatment of Ishmael as a first-person character, which takes place approximately at the point of overlap between Stewart's "two Moby-Dicks" reveals a connection between the new narrative situation and the genesis and reconception of the work. This novel thus contains both formations of the first-person narrative situation—both the tight and the loose connection of the narrating self to the experiencing self. The author was quite unrestricted in his creation of the narrative situation; he subjected it completely to the narrative requirements of the individual scene.

Point 2:

The posterior relationship of the narrating self to the experiencing self would seem to be so self-evident as to need no further elucidation. Yet the manner in which this circumstance is realized in the novel produces several important factors which significantly influence the reader's imaginative process. In the text this relationship is tangibly expressed in the narrative distance, which in the first-person novel measures the temporal separation of the narrating self from the experiencing self, that is, of the narrative act from the experience.

The narrative distance in *Moby-Dick* becomes different on or near the spot which was established by Stewart and which evidenced a transformation in the appearance of Ishmael. The passage at the beginning of the novel established the time span of "some years" as the narrative distance in the "first Moby-Dick." Speculation about how many years are concealed behind this statement is less important than the fact that the narrator apparently does not regard it as a very long span of time. This view is supported by the use of the present tense in the sentence: "It [sailing about] is a way I have of driving off the spleen, and regulating the circulation." The narrator implies here that the original motivation of his voyage could affect him again in the same way even now. A sea voyage of the kind described, however, can hardly still be the wish of an older man who, like the first-person narrator in later chapters, has already grown accustomed to desk work.

In connection with the encounter of the Pequod with the Samuel Enderby the narrator foreshadows the fact that once afterwards he again boarded the Samuel Enderby, somewhere off the coast of Patagonia. This last visit, however, took place "long, very long after old Ahab touched her planks with his ivory heel . . ." (CI, p. 441). This visit on board the Samuel Enderby must have occurred a long time before the first day in the life of the first-person narrator when he sat down to write the story of his voyage on the Pequod. Yet from the standpoint of the second meeting the first one already lies in his eyes very far in the past, "long, very long after." In order to estimate the narrative distance from these data, this "very long" span of time between the two meetings would not be sufficient. One would have to take into account the time which passed between the Patagonian voyage and the beginning of his work recording the voyage of the Pequod. No reader will make this complicated calculation in his imagination. In any case the reader's imagination will certainly register the important fact that now the voyage on the Pequod seems to lie further back in the narrator's memory than at the beginning of the novel, where it was only a few years distant. The new narrative distance can hardly be expressed now as "some years." There is no indication of a correspondingly long duration of the narrative process itself; under certain circumstances this could explain the shift. On the contrary, everything indicates that the fictional process of composition corresponds in duration to the real composition of the novel.

The initial fictional conception, the intellectual frame in which the author holds the novel's potential material at the moment of composition, must have undergone a change. It is striking that this change can be traced approximately from the point where the thorough reworking of the novel supposedly commenced. The original perspective was a close-up view, which usually serves to present adventurous but not all too unusual events. The new perspective is a remote view. Only this made it possible for the narrative to capture and present the colossal, the uncanny, the incomprehensible, the supernatural in all its inherent symbolic power. This midway increase in the narrative distance is especially important because it reveals a change in the author's attitude—a change for which he himself could hardly have accounted at the moment of composition. The designation of the two narrative distances is expressed vaguely, in adjectives for the most part. It seems likely that the author did not consciously keep track of the narrative distance; it arose naturally as a function of his basic conception of the novel. This becomes even clearer when one compares these indirect indications of the time with the explicit date given by the narrator to fix the time level of the narrative act. The date appears in one of the chapters on "cetology," as the general sections on the whale and whaling are called by American critics: "this blessed minute (fifteen and a quarter minutes past one o'clock P.M. of this sixteenth day of December, A.D. 1851) . . ." (LXXXV, p. 367). A pecularity of this temporal designation of the narrative act—perhaps it follows Sterne's example in *Tristram Shandy*—is the minute pedantry. It challenges the reader to imagine analogous temporal precision for the whole duration of the narrative act. The date, December 16, 1851, is also striking because it names a day on which the novel had already appeared. This is even more remarkable in that the English first edition bears the date December 16, 1850.[8] A letter written to Evert Duykinck three days before this date shows that Melville actually was working on *Moby-Dick* in the winter of 1850.[9] As long as no explanation can be found for the 1851 date of the American edition, one will have to view the 1850 date of the English edition as the correct one. It should be noted, however, that the English editors were at times quite arbitrary in their handling of the text; it is possible that they are responsible for the correction of the date.[10]

The temporal level of the narrative act is frequently designated in less precise terms, such as "now," "this day," "at the present," and so forth. Such indications are naturally quite numerous in the chapters on cetology, where the narrator reports not on his past experience but on his present knowledge of the whale. "Not even at the present day has the original prestige of the Sperm Whale, as fearfully distinguished from all other species of the leviathan, died out of the minds of the whalemen as a body" (XLI, p. 177).

During long stretches of the novel the first-person narrator appears only as an author who sits at his desk and assembles scholarship on the whale from numerous books. In Chapters CII to CV there are no references at all to the Pequod and to Ishmael. The experiencing self disappears completely behind the narrating self. Here, too, the experiencing self no longer appears as the primary source, the informant, of the narrating self; it is emphasized more than once that the narrator acquired his theoretical knowledge of cetology only after the voyage on the Pequod, by dint of toilsome research. The chapters on cetology belong to the realm of the narrating self; they are an expression of its interests and knowledge at the time of the narrative process.

One can thus distinguish between two terraces of action which are separated from each other by the narrative distance. On the first terrace the predominating medium is the experiencing self,

Ishmael; on the second terrace the narrating self predominates. In the presentation of the action on the Pequod and the experiences of Ishmael there are continual references to the terrace of the narrative self, to the narrative process, and to cetology. As a result both terraces are almost always realized simultaneously in the reader's imagination, while both strands of action appear temporally separated by the narrative distance. Allusions to the narrator's experiences between the voyage on the Pequod and the narrative act also serve to characterize the narrative distance. A number of such episodes, which are never more than intimated, fill in the time span between the two terraces of action. In this way the identity of the experiencing self with the narrating self is reaffirmed; the unity of the individual is concretely portrayed. In most of these episodes the self still appears in a form which has more in common with the experiencing self than with the narrating self. This figure of the self appears as a sailor and global vagabond on his visit aboard the Samuel Enderby off the coast of Patagonia (CI, p. 441); as a yarn-spinning sailor in Lima, surrounded by a crowd of Spanish admirers (LIV, p. 241); and finally in a similar manner for King Tranquo of Tranque, ruler of the Solomon Islands (CII, p. 446). These episodes occupy by far the greatest part of the time span corresponding to the narrative distance. Only a relatively short segment of the narrative distance is dedicated to his cetological occupations and his subsequent activities as a writer. The attempt of the narrator to show his credentials as an experienced geologist by referring to his work as a stonemason and as a digger of canals and wells does not quite fit this picture. It is probably meant as a part of the ironical treatment of science which comes to light here and there in the cetology chapters (CIV, p. 453).

The impletion of the time which separates the narrating self from the experiencing self makes this expanse become concretely visible. It renews and strengthens the identity of the two manifestations of the self. Both processes have an effect on the reader's imagination. The detailed designation of the narrative process emphatically places the center of orientation in the narrating self. Because of the demonstrated identity of the narrating self and the experiencing self, however, the center of orientation can be shifted back to the now-and-here of the latter. The frequent passages of scenic presentation therefore do not perceptibly violate the reader's illusion expectancy. This kind of orientation can be observed quite clearly in the chapter "The Try-Works" (XCVI). The chapter begins with a present-tense factual statement which initially leaves the center of orientation in the narrating self. In the subsequent description of operations on board the Pequod the voice of the narrating self still remains audible. Only the paragraph beginning "By midnight the works were in full operation . . ." brings about a change. The scene emerges more and more forcefully as the immediate presentation of the present experience of Ishmael, who is standing at the helm, gazing into the ghostly fire beneath the blubber-pots. A sudden reminder of the narrator transfers the center of orientation from Ishmael's now-and-here at the helm back to the narrating self at his desk.

In both the authorial and the first-person novel narrative conventions have evolved for the use of scenic presentation. Events far in the narrator's past can be presented scenically with no detriment whatsoever to the illusion of the work. Nevertheless, some authors make such literal use of the narrative situation of the first-person novel that they employ a predominantly report-like mode of narration throughout the novel. Truman Capote's *The Grass Harp* is a first-person novel in which the voice of the narrating self is never fully drowned out by scenic presentation. With the exception of a few lyrical descriptions the novel is written in a distinctly colloquial style. One almost always has the impression that the author is speaking before an audience. It is especially characteristic of the first-person narrator occasionally to incorporate the direct discourse of a figure into his report. This is illustrated by the sentence "But Riley said Sheriff, you're after the wrong party" from the following passage:

Afterwards, Rose was sent off to a place on the Gulf Coast, an institution, and she may still be living there, at least I've never heard that she died. Now Riley and his uncle Horace Holton couldn't get on. One night he stole Horace's Oldsmobile and drove out to the Dance-N-Dine with Mamie Curtiss: she was fast as lightning, and maybe five years older than Riley, who was not more than fifteen at the time. Well, Horace heard they were at the Dance-N-Dine and got the Sheriff to drive him out there: he said he was going to teach Riley a lesson and have him arrested. But Riley said Sheriff, you're after the wrong party. Right there in front of a crowd he accused his uncle of stealing money. . . .

(The Grass Harp, p. 33)

Point 3:

Some further inferences can be made from the personal identification of the narrating self with the experiencing self, and from the way in which the narrative distance is designated. The experiencing self, Ishmael, cannot foresee his fate. With no misgivings he enlists on the Pequod for a long whaling voyage. Even before the ship sets sail, however, the first signs appear which put the coming voyage under an unfavorable star. And the closer the ship comes to the scene of the unsuspected catastrophe, the oftener appear these omens of a dire ending. Ishmael mirrors the mood of the crew. He surrenders more and more to the temptation to see behind every unusual phenomenon an ominous meaning, a prefiguration of terrible events in store for the ship. Despite this the catastrophe finally befalls the victims with all the terror of the unexpected.

For the narrating self, separated from these events by the narrative distance, the voyage of the Pequod must appear in a panoramic view from its departure to its sinking. Every first-person narrator who reports events from a similar temporal remove actually has this complete knowledge of the events. Yet first-person narrators only rarely make prefigurative comments which anticipate the conclusion and resolution of the conflict. The narrator of *Moby-Dick*, too, does not allow the reader to know in advance the conclusion of the ship's voyage. The number of prefigurations is itself quite small in comparison to the innumerable presentiments, prophecies, and supposedly ominous happenings. All the narrator's prefigurations refer to secondary aspects of the action and in each case anticipate the narrative by only a short span of time. Sometimes an event which at first Ishmael does not fully understand is reported with an immediate explanation of what was later learned. The story of Queequeg's life is interpolated at the point when Queequeg first tries to tell it to Ishmael. Ishmael must admit that he only understood the meaning of Queequeg's words when he had later become familiar with the broken phraseology of this "savage." The narrator makes widest use of his foreknowledge of the action in presenting the ship's officers and harpooners. In the two chapters entitled "Knights and Squires" (XXVI, XXVII) the narrator gives these figures all the attributes which they reveal in the course of the voyage. Nor does he hesitate to anticipate later events in order to illustrate these characteristics. This narrative stance uses prefigurations to supplement and deepen the first impression of a given figure. The first appearance of Ahab, the captain of the Pequod, is the clearest illustration of this technique. The reader first experiences with Ishmael the initial appearance of Ahab on the upper deck of the Pequod. Immediately, however, the narrator supplements the portrayal of this first impression. He adds to it opinions and statements which were uttered by the crew members later in the voyage, after this point in time (XXVIII, p. 120 ff).

The first-person narrator does not always evince that superiority in surveying the whole which the reader can expect of him in this narrative situation. There are several shifts in the basic plan, later emphases which are not anticipated in the preceding parts of the novel. There are initial references which are never taken up and exploited. The historically demonstrable change of the original conception of the novel infringes on the unity of the final execution. Here, too, these shifts in the basic plan are especially evident when they encompass both the beginning, that is, the "first Moby-Dick," and the main part of the work. George R. Stewart's article "The Two Moby-Dicks" contains further details and evidence related to this problem. Stewart explains the shift as the merging of two different versions or of two levels which were rewritten to different degrees. This, of course, does not affect the structural diagnosis that the novel's structure of meaning was deflected at one point and received a new accentuation. One possible motivation for this narrative change of direction is a peculiar kind of behavior on the part of the narrator. The first-person narrator in *Moby-Dick* has a strong commitment to the moment of narration. Only gradually is it possible for him to apprehend the potential patterns of meaning and the symbolic power of the images. As the narrative progresses whole new accents and interpretations often arise which were not foreseen originally.

The narrating self seems to reflect rather faithfully the conceptional and creative work of the real author. It is not surprising, then, that this narrating self may dissociate itself from its proper role in the narrative situation in order directly to take up a new idea which gives the narrative a new turn. In this case the narrator of the third-person novel can make use of the motif of consulting with the reader about the best way to continue the novel. In the first-person novel this motif occurs less often, but it can be introduced there, as Laurence Sterne shows in *Tristram Shandy*. George R. Stewart calls attention to a passage in *Moby-Dick* which he calls an "insight passage."[11] He believes that it contains the germ of the whole rewritten version. In this passage the real author's conception and planning of the novel become visible. No attempt is made to disguise it as part of the narrative act. Stewart also noted the striking isolation of this passage in the context of the chapter and the quite ambiguous syntactic connection to what came before. For this reason he surmises that it was originally a memorandum of Melville's which the author incorporated into the narrative without alteration. If one keeps in mind the varying modes of appearance of the narrating self, however, it is not absolutely necessary to regard the passage as a curiosum which has more or less by chance come into the narrative context. Here, as elsewhere, the first-person narrator extends the limits of the reader's illusion expectancy so far that only the narrator's use of the pronoun "I" remains to distinguish this form from that of the third-person novel. In such a passage the narrating self distances itself so far from the experiencing self that the former no longer pretends to report the latter's experience from memory. The narrating self's conception of the novel, which only receives its final content in the course of the narrative act, is here expressed directly, with no further narrative guise. Strictly speaking this inverts the arrangement which places the narrative act in a relationship of posteriority to the narrated action in the reader's illusion expectancy. Examples of such inversions were also noted in the authorial novel.

The "insight passage" is interpolated into the narration of Ishmael's first meeting with the two Quakers, Peleg and Bildad, on whose ship he wants to serve:

> Now, Bildad, like Peleg, and indeed many other Nantucketers, was a Quaker . . . some of these same Quakers are the most sanguinary of all sailors and whale-hunters. They are fighting Quakers; they are Quakers with a vengeance.
>
> So that there are instances among them of men, who, named with Scripture names—a singularly common fashion on the island—and in childhood naturally imbibing the stately dramatic thee and thou of the Quaker idiom; still, from the audacious, daring, and boundless adventure of their subsequent lives, strangely blend with these unoutgrown peculiarities, a thousand bold dashes of character, not unworthy a Scandinavian sea-king, or a poetical Pagan Roman. And when these things unite in a man of greatly superior natural force, with a globular brain and a ponderous heart; who has also by the stillness and seclusion of many night-watches in the remotest waters, and beneath constellations never seen here at the north, been led to think untraditionally and independently; receiving all nature's sweet or savage impressions fresh from her own virgin voluntary and confiding breast, and thereby chiefly, but with some help from accidental advantages, to learn a bold and nervous lofty language—that man makes one in a whole nation's census—a mighty pageant creature, formed for noble tragedies. Nor will it at all detract from him, dramatically regarded, if either by birth or other circumstances, he have what seems a half wilful overruling morbidness at the bottom of his nature. For all men tragically great are made so through a certain morbidness.
>
> (XVI, p. 72–73)

In the context of the chapter this preview of the personality and character of Captain Ahab is conspicuous by more than its content alone. It is remarkable for its verbal form, especially its sentence structure, which clearly emphasizes the most important perception of this paragraph—Ahab as "one in a whole nation's census . . . formed for noble tragedies." This view of the novel's central figure—a view which Stewart sees as the impetus for the whole rewriting of the novel—thus reveals its incomplete integration into the report of the first-person narrator.

Point 4:

For the interpretation of the novel a further inference can be made from the narrative distance. The narrating self is older than the experiencing self by the time span of the narrative distance. During this time he has become more mature; his attitude and way of life have become different. It should be possible to demonstrate the extent to which this circumstance is realized in the person of the first-person narrator in *Moby-Dick*.

In *Moby-Dick* the experiencing as well as the narrating self appear as primary sources of information. The narrating self registers his experiences, his valuations, and interpretations of the events, just as the experiencing self. For this reason a tension or opposition often arises between the experiencing self's accompanying valuation of an event as it happens, on the one hand, and the valuation provided by the narrating self, on the other. The narrating self, however, usually succeeds in putting himself back into the experiences of the experiencing self far enough that this tension does not emerge. In many first-person novels no narrative use whatsoever is made of this potential tension. But whenever the narrating self is clearly profiled, as he is in *Moby-Dick*, this potential tension between the experiencing self and the narrating self becomes an important structural element of the novel. Quite frequently the reports and scenes of Ishmael's voyage come into a peculiar contrast with the sections on cetology and with the narrating self's reports about his writing. Ishmael's unreflected experiences appear in close proximity to the narrating self's biological observations on the whale. Everything worth knowing about the whale is here assembled from contemporary sources and actual reports of whaling voyages. Individual phenomena are always arranged according to their place in a general pattern; the unique particulars strive for documentation in an all-encompassing and systematic whole. Alongside Ishmael's perspective in the whaleboat, as he feels the spout of the hunted whale in his face, stands the perspective of the zealous scholar. In contrast to Ishmael he sits at his desk, classifies and categorizes the species, and neatly displays his findings to the reader. At the same time there is more than one ironic jab taken at scientific overclassification. The last chapters of the novel portray the encounter with the whale and the supernatural terror which overcomes Ishmael and the crew at the sight of Moby Dick. This may be compared with the same theme as it appears in the enlightened tone of the narrating self in an earlier chapter:

> Alone, in such remotest waters, that though you sailed a thousand miles, and passed a thousand shores, you would not come to any chiselled hearthstone, or aught hospitable beneath that part of the sun; in such latitudes and longitudes, pursuing too such a calling as he does, the whaleman is wrapped by influences all tending to make his fancy pregnant with many a mighty birth.
>
> No wonder, then, that ever gathering volume from the mere transit over the widest watery spaces, the outblown rumors of the White Whale did in the end incorporate with themselves all manner of morbid hints, and half-formed foetal suggestions of supernatural agencies, which eventually invested Moby Dick with new terrors unborrowed from anything that visibly appears. So that in many cases such a panic did he finally strike, that few who by those rumors, at least, had heard of the White Whale, few of those hunters were willing to encounter the perils of his jaw.
>
> (XLI, p. 177)

Here the narrative function of the narrating self in relation to the experiencing self is the same as that performed by the enlightened schoolmaster's narrating self in Theodor Storm's novella *Der Schimmelreiter*. Storm's schoolmaster, however, is a frame-narrator who is not identical with any of the experiencing figures. In *Moby-Dick* this narrative relationship, which serves to screen off the supernatural elements of the fictional world from the empirical world of the reader, is united in the figure of the first-person narrator.

The chapter in which the narrator attacks the legendary phenomenon of the White Whale with his Enlightenmentlike armament is immediately followed by perhaps the most original chapter in the entire novel, "The Whiteness of the Whale" (XLII). It begins with the somewhat ambiguous statement: "What the white whale was to Ahab, has been hinted; what, at times, he was to me, as yet remains unsaid." And then follows that series of comparisons and images, all revolving about the symbolism of the whale's white color, which reveal anything but an enlightened observer. To what does "at times" refer? To Ishmael of the Pequod; to Ishmael the global vagabond who tries to free himself from the experience of his meeting with the white whale; or to the narrating self who sits at his desk behind his books on cetology? Here the identity of the narrating self with the experiencing self is apparently complete once again. To be sure, Ishmael's original experience receives its verbal and intellectual form from the narrating self; but the experience retains the valuation which it was originally given by the experiencing self.

Sometimes the narrator does not even wait for a subsequent opportunity, such as a chapter on cetology, to comment on Ishmael's experiences. He intrudes immediately, like an authorial narrator. One day a glistening cream-colored mass is sighted in the water. All boats are set out and approach the spot in great suspense. The mass, whose white color had caused the crew to assume it was Moby Dick, proves to be a squid:

As with a low sucking sound it slowly disappeared again, Starbuck still gazing at the agitated waters where it had sunk, with a wild voice exclaimed—"Almost rather had I seen Moby Dick and fought him, than to have seen thee, thou white ghost!"

"What was it, Sir?" asked Flask.

"The great live squid, which, they say, few whale-ships ever beheld, and returned to their ports to tell of it."

But Ahab said nothing; turning to his boat, he sailed back to the vessel; the rest as silently following.

Whatever superstitions the sperm whalemen in general have connected with the sight of this object, certain it is, that a glimpse of it being so very unusual, that circumstance has gone far to invest it with portentousness. So rarely is it beheld, that though one and all of them declare it to be the largest animated thing in the ocean, yet very few of them have any but the most vague ideas concerning it true nature and form. (LIX, pp. 276–77)

Does Ishmael, who rows "silently" back to the ship with the rest of the crew, also regard Starbuck's omen simply as a superstition? Starbuck's belief in portents comes up against the narrator's enlightened view in the next paragraph. The narrating self encounters the experiencing self with the same skeptical irony often observed between a frame-narrator and his previous narrator. A kind of tension arises which is similar to that of the authorial novel. Here one can see the opposition which results as the narrating self separates itself by time, experience, and mood from the experiencing self.

In each of the four points according to which the first-person novel has been treated here, striking similarities with the authorial novel have come to light. The limits of observation established for the narrator by the experiencing self are frequently transgressed. In this way the narrator makes use of a narrative stance which is actually the province of the authorial narrator. Even where the narrative distance is clearly marked in the narrative, both reportlike narration and scenic presentation are considered— as in the third-person novel—to be fully and equally suited to the narrative situation. The voice of the first-person narrator in passages with distinct scenic presentation is just as difficult to perceive as the voice of the authorial narrator in similar passages of a third-person novel. In the guise and realization of both novel forms traces could be found of the original process of conception and composition. Between narrating and experiencing self a kind of tension could be observed which is similar to the tension in the third-person novel between the authorial narrator and the fictional world. Parallels between the authorial novel and the first-person novel are all the more revealing in view of the established relationship between them which even makes a gradual transition possible from one to the other.

In addition to the narrative conventions of the authorial novel a further convention appears in the first-person novel: the narrator alleges himself a figure in the fictional world. As a rule this new convention requires a more complex guise for the narrative situation. This more disciplined act of narration is not generally required in the authorial novel with its greater narrative freedom. As a result the first-person novel has always been a hunting ground rich in curiosities for those who collect instances of excessive and false motivation. On closer inspection these false motivations almost always prove to be attempts to compensate for transgressions of first-person narrative conventions. To infer the "abnormity of the first-person novel" because of the frequency of such errors, however, is an uncritical and hasty judgment.[12] On the same grounds one could speak of the abnormity of the third-person narrative, for many third-person novels often fail to observe strictly the point of view established by the narrative guise.

There is a widely held but questionable view that the first-person form in a narrative allows one to interpret the narrative primarily as an autobiographical statement of the author. Hildegard Zeller seems to tend in this direction, for her interpretations lead again and again to the insidious conclusion: first-person narrator equals author.[13] From the standpoint of poetic theory it is difficult to understand why the identification of the narrating self with a figure of the novel, namely the experiencing self, should be taken so literally. The third-person novel's comparable claim of authenticity for its narrated material is almost always taken for what it is—a part of the quasi-real guise which has become a common convention of this narrative situation. Käte Hamburger draws, basically, the same false conclusion. As an autobiographical and thus historical document, according to Hamburger, the first-person narrative theoretically ceases to share the fictionality of narrated worlds. The first-person narrator, according to Hamburger, presents itself as nonfictive; the narrated material is thus placed in the realm of the historical, in the presenting (rather than the presented) world, the reality of the author and the reader.[14]

The identification of the first-person narrator with a figure of the fictional world represents the first-person novel's characteristic means of verifying the narrated matter. Moreover, this striving for verification and authentication is a basic concern of all narrative art. In the first-person novel this desire for verification is achieved by extending the fictional reality to include the narrative process. The incorporation of the narrative process into the realm of the fictional world causes the reader to forget the division into a presenting and a presented reality. Everything, even the narrative process, appears with a fictive claim to a quasi-real existence. The narrative process no longer represents the real author's actual process of creation; rather, the original creative act now undergoes a dramatization, which is presented in a figure of the novel. Both the dramatization and the transposition to a fictional figure establish the fact that the narrative process in the first-person novel is a part of the fiction. Käte Hamburger's view that the first-person narrative stands as a nonfictive form of narrative in the realm of the historical is thus untenable. Her attempt to locate the first-person narrative "between the fictional genres of epic and dramatic poetry and the purely existential genre of lyric poetry"[15] cannot be upheld. The theoretical position of the first-person narrative can only be sought in the realm of the novel. This investigation has demonstrated the position of the first-person novel between the authorial novel and the figural novel.

Käte Hamburger maintains that in the first-person narrative the epic preterite possesses only the imaginative value of the past. This is just as untenable as her attempt to view the epic preterite in the third-person novel exclusively as an expression of the present. In both cases the situation is similar. In the first-person as well as the third-person novel the imaginative value of the epic preterite is determined by the specific narrative situation and by the resulting position of the reader's center of orientation. In both forms of the novel the epic preterite can possess the imaginative value of the present as well as that of the past.

IV

THE FIGURAL NOVEL

THE FIGURAL NARRATIVE SITUATION and its variant, the neutral narrative situation, were described in the chapter "The Narrative Situation and the Epic Preterite." The following characteristic features were established: withdrawal of the author; predominance of scenic presentation; the reader's center of orientation fixed in the now-and-here of a novel figure or of an imaginary observer on the scene of the action; and the possibility of giving the epic preterite the imaginative value of the present. Unless expressly stated otherwise, the term figural novel will refer in this chapter to both the figural and neutral narrative situations.

Like the authorial novel and the first-person novel, the figural novel is only rarely realized in a consistent, typical form. Like the first-person novel, the figural novel also tends to include authorial elements in the figural narrative situation. Of course, the situation of the individual reader will in turn determine what can still be considered authorial. In a scenically presented section even a personally colored or biased epithet, a few lines of more highly compressed report, or a slight prefiguration may be regarded by some readers as authorial intrusion. An authorial narrative situation will then be concretized in the imaginations of such readers. Narrative economy, which is always an author's concern, may often make it necessary to forego the sometimes rather elaborate presentation of material in a figural narrative situation. If "stage directions" must be given which are too complicated to be mirrored in a figure's consciousness, or if it would be too pedantic to transpose some narrative remark into scenic presentation, then the author can have brief recourse to an authorial narrative situation. The complete "dramatization" of the novel, if such a thing must absolutely be attempted, can only be purchased at the expense of a large number of narrative techniques and conventions.

Nevertheless, even in its consistent type-form the figural novel can be realized; it should not be overlooked in a theory of the possible forms of the novel. There is thus reason to protest the fact that such well-known theoreticians of the novel as Käte Friedemann, Robert Petsch, and others have called the figural novel a formal folly, a form of non-form, or a degenerate form. It was already observed that in a long narrative work a totally figural situation is only rarely desirable. The kind of objectivity demanded by Friedrich Spielhagen presupposes a degree of illusion expectancy which the reader does not have. What Spielhagen and his followers attempted can be attained with a much less drastic curtailment and limitation of the narrative process. Even during the reading of an authorial novel one can observe an effect of presentness as complete as that in the figural narrative situation. This occurs, for example, in long dialogue scenes where the authorial narrator makes only a few, short comments and "stage directions." This clearly indicates that the figural novel is basically only the consistent employment of a technique which arises for brief stretches even in an authorial novel.

A successful figural novel, too, need not depend on the extreme logical realization of a typical narrative situation. It depends, rather, on the wise use of all the narrative conventions which this form can offer the author. Only gradually has the figural novel isolated its own peculiar conventions from those of the authorial novel. The extent to which the stage, the film, and the closet drama have favored this process has not yet been clarified. The differing attitudes of Otto Ludwig and Oskar Walzel, as presented in the first chapter, clearly indicate that a development —a proliferation of the form of the figural novel—has taken place since the turn of the century.

An important narrative convention in the figural novel is the neutralization of a number of narrative elements. In the context of a figurally or neutrally presented scene certain potentially authorial elements completely cease to refer to or indicate the act of narration. This applies to the *verba dicendi*; to the short "stage directions" often strewn into the dialogue; and possibly to the relatively objective report which closely accompanies the action of the scene. This narrative convention makes it possible to bring about the effect of a figural narrative situation without completely relinquishing traditional narrative style and forms.

Several objections which have been raised concerning the figural novel have already been discussed in the first chapter. In view of the overwhelming number of literally successful figural novels, a fundamental defense of this form seems unnecessary. Most of the third-person novels of Henry James, John Dos Passos, Ernest Hemingway, John Steinbeck, Virginia Woolf, Aldous Huxley, and many others can serve as examples of successful figural novels.

It is necessary, however, to discuss briefly the most recent objection to the figural novel—that of Wolfgang Kayser in his article "Die Anfänge des modernen Romans im 18. Jahrhundert und seine heutige Krise."[1] Kayser voices his misgivings about the figural novel in connection with his very illuminating and sensitive treatment of the "fictive narrator," that is, the authorial narrator. Kayser examines the narrative stance and the possibilities of disguising the author as authorial narrator. For the most part these observations confirm the conclusions made in this study, without knowledge of Kayser's article, concerning the authorial narrator and the peculiar narrative situation of the authorial novel. Kayser cannot be supported, however, when he attempts to place the type of the authorial novel (including the first-person novel) above the figural novel or when he attempts to call into question the figural novel itself. "The death of the narrator is the death of the novel."[2] Kayser is certainly not trying to abolish the figural novel. He is concerned, rather, with showing how seldom the extreme employment of a figural narrative situation leads to an authentic literary creation.

Since the turn of the century the figural novel has enjoyed ever-growing popularity among authors and readers. This popularity can obviously be traced in large measure to the discovery of the human consciousness as an object of literary presentation.[3] The various forms and possibilities which are available for the literary creation of consciousness will be treated in the chapter on the presentation of consciousness. It should be emphasized that even the material which offers itself to the author in the realm of consciousness still requires the creation of a form and structure of meaning. It must still be ordered structurally and formed into a unity. Precisely the apparent formlessness, the apparent fortuitousness which distinguishes the arrangement of material as the content of consciousness makes the task of the author especially challenging. Here his creative efforts delve into much deeper levels, into the most inconspicuous ramifications of detail, while external events come to him largely in an already established form. In comparison to the authorial novel the figural novel seems better suited to the unusual task of rendering the contents of consciousness. Especially the figural novel in the precise sense—with a character acting as figural medium and bearer of consciousness—seems to accomplish the task more easily and more convincingly. Frequently the subtle substance of consciousness evades the techniques of presentation which are available to an authorial narrator as he reports from his remote point of view.

The figural novel chosen for interpretation here is not intended to represent an extreme or strictly consistent realization of this novel form. Henry James's novel *The Ambassadors* manifests a whole series of authorial features. In the case of this novel it is also possible to show that James selected the narrative situation by carefully considering the various possibilities and the material he wished to present.

The figural novel has been treated here almost exclusively as a form of the "novel of consciousness." It should be added that objective-scenic presentation of external events is also encompassed by this novel form. In such works the extreme dialogue scene usually prevails; this is a characteristic feature of the neutral mode of presentation. Ernest Hemingway's "The Killers" is an example of neutral presentation. The mediation of fictional reality no longer exhibits an actual medium. All traces of a process of narration are eliminated. The attempt to approximate the form and effect of a play can clearly be seen in John Steinbeck's "play novelettes" *Burning Bright* and *Of Mice and Men*. In his preface to *Burning Bright* the author explains that it was his express intention to create in these novelettes works which could immediately be presented on the stage.[4] The parts of the work not written in dialogue would then become extensive stage directions. Steinbeck's experiment is a revealing one, for it illustrates the highly analogous relationships that exist between the dramatic imaginative process and the reader's imaginative process in a figural narrative situation.

The Ambassadors

Henry James's artistic development into the mature creative period of his major phase, in which he wrote *The Wings of the Dove* (1902), *The Ambassadors* (1903), and *The Golden Bowl* (1904),[5] exemplifies the movement of an author toward sharper self-discipline of his creative talent and toward more and more conscious selection of forms and structural techniques. To trace this development of the author would be especially fruitful, since it drew James further and further away from an initial tendency to compose his novels in an authorial form and led him ever closer to the figural form, with the result that James wrote his great novels of the late period predominantly in this form. From among these three novels one work had to be chosen for interpretation here. In addition to those reasons for selecting *The Ambassadors* which were cited in the preceding section, it was of no small significance that for this novel James himself wrote a detailed scenario, which has been published, together with the *Notebooks*, by F. O. Matthiessen and Kenneth B. Murdock.[6] One thus has access to four stages in the writing and evaluation of the novel which reveal the work in various phases of its composition and, ultimately, Henry James himself in an act of personally criticizing and evaluating the work: the entries in the *Notebooks*; the scenario to the novel; the finished novel; and the "Preface" which James wrote for *The Ambassadors* several years after its completion. James wrote "Prefaces" for all those stories and novels which were included in the final edition during his lifetime of the majority of his works, the New York Edition, published in the years 1907 to 1917. An imposing number of years thus lies between the writing of the early novels, in particular, and the corresponding "Preface." It is for this reason that the Henry James of the "Prefaces" frequently does his early novels an injustice and that several of his statements concerning the conception and writing of these novels are not absolutely valid. This reservation in regard to the "Prefaces" is only partially applicable to *The Ambassadors*, since in this case a shorter span of time separates the writing of the novel from the writing of the "Preface," and since this novel was written in a spirit which was already largely congenial to the spirit which gave rise to the "Prefaces." Nevertheless, even for *The Ambassadors* we can still detect inconsistencies between the entries in the *Notebooks* and the "Preface." Such inconsistencies, however, will not be of great importance for this study.

The report in the "Preface" concerning the genesis of the novel testifies to the fact that James chose the narrative situation for *The Ambassadors* only after thorough consideration. In this regard it seems highly significant that James found the first-person form totally inadequate for his purposes. The fact that he was fully aware of the characteristic structural feature of the first-person novel—the identity but divided function of the narrating self and the experiencing self—is apparent from his characterization of the first-person narrator as "hero and historian . . . with the double privilege of subject and object."[7] His main objection to the first-person novel is that it is "foredoomed to looseness."[8] Naturally, one cannot agree with this statement unconditionally, though it seems understandable that a first-person novel in the manner of *David Copperfield*, where a ready-made plot structure, the life of the first-person narrator, is employed to establish a gallery of characters or to hold together a collection of episodes, had to appear barely serviceable for James's architectonic plans. His first objection to the form of the first-person novel is connected with the second, the "terrible *fluidity* of self-revelation"[9] with which the first-person narrative unfolds. The aim in *The Ambassadors* was to present in Strether, the central figure of the novel, mental processes which are produced by a highly delicate situation, portraying them in the undelineated state of the first moment; in their unresolved interconflict; and in their manifold concatenations with momentary moods, thoughts, and encounters. In the autobiographical account of a first-person narrator all this would appear in the perspective of that which is permanently terminated, of that which is past. Moreover, the first-person narrator uses a rather coarse crayon to sketch a picture of his past. He employs a quick, bold stroke to compress and conclude processes which took place slowly and with no fixed line of development. Neither of these techniques would achieve the delicate shades, the bizarre contours which the mental portrait of Strether requires. They would obscure "certain precious discriminations"[10] which were of importance to James. The figural form of the novel seemed to James the remedy for these deficiencies. In Lambert Strether, Henry James found an ideal figural medium, to which he could confidently entrust the crucial position at the window through which the fictional world is viewed.

Moby-Dick is a novel of action full of adventurous occurrences. The extraordinary and the supernatural enter directly into the realistic portrayal of the routine of the whale hunt. In this way the most disparate elements can come into conjunction on the same page of the novel. This circumstance requires the assimilating, harmonizing, and binding power of a narrator whose narrative distance serves to create a unified structure. In *The Ambassadors*, on the other hand, one is confronted with a thoroughly homogeneous but all the more volatile material which, in contrast to the adventurous happenings in the foreground of *Moby-Dick*, does not cry out for a narrative structure in the form of a report, but rather seems to deny such a form. In *Moby-Dick* the experiences of the soul are projected in colossal images against the grandiose background of expansive oceans. In *The Ambassadors* the author is faced with the task of creating adequate expression for slight and highly subtle movements in the consciousness of the central figure—movements which are frequently attended only by minute gestures or by a carefully selected expression in the dialogue. In this case the compressed summarization characteristic of an authorial report would be equivalent to simplification, relaxation of the mental polarities, and possibly even banalization. The reader must be given the illusion of being able to follow the mental processes of the central figure directly, without the obtrusive mediative presence of the narrator. Henry James achieved this with outstanding success in *The Ambassadors*.

The apparent remnants of authorial narration in *The Ambassadors* will be discussed first. This will be followed by an examination of the manner in which James succeeds in dramatizing the consciousness of a character using the figural method.

In his preface to *The Ambassadors* Henry James admits that despite his efforts to create a "scenic" narrative, he departed from this aim several times in the course of the novel. In his own way, and with the appropriate reservations, he then acknowledges the fact that the exclusive use of scenic presentation in a novel is not always worth the associated surrender of other presentational techniques: "I have . . . not failed to note how . . . the finest proprieties and charms of the non-scenic may, under the right hand for them, still keep their intelligibility and assert their office" (*Prefaces*, p. 325). On the very first page of the novel the narrator steps forward with an unmistakably authorial "I." Overt designation of the narrator, however, is not maintained. His presence is only perceptible in comments not unlike stage directions which are kept quite impersonal. An occasional epithet ("poor Strether," p. 172);[11] now and then a quick interpretation of an event, but without drawing the personal presence of the narrator into conscious view of the reader ("Strether's reading of such matters was, it must be owned, confused," p. 206)—none of these will succeed in suspending in the majority of readers the impression of figural presentation.

The author was confronted with a difficult problem in his attempt to present Strether's mental processes in a predominantly figural but not authorial style. What stylistic technique could create the illusion that these mental processes, which are the actual dramatic action of the novel, become known to the reader by means of a direct glimpse into the thoughts and feelings of Strether and not by means of a narrator's report? Henry James's presentation of consciousness still belongs to the generation before James Joyce. Although James was not unreceptive to the psychological findings of his brother, William James, concerning the inner laws which govern consciousness, he was still far removed from realizing these inner laws—in his narrative technique as well as in his language—by means of autonomous presentation of consciousness such as that attempted later by James Joyce. For the processes of consciousness Henry James employs a style still analogous to literary language, to elevated prose with intact syntax and orthodox word formation. Pictorially one could imagine James's method of presenting consciousness in this way: he executes a cross section through Strether's consciousness at a height where the content of this consciousness already appears formulated as thoughts expressed in their traditional verbal forms. In this way occasional comments of the author are possible with no change in the stylistic level. Consequently, no attention is drawn to the momentarily authorial narrative situation. Here, as everywhere in the realm of literary art, one cannot fix with objective certainty the point beyond which the immediate perception and experience of that which is being narrated begins to include a simultaneous awareness of the narrative process itself.

In *The Ambassadors* a figural narrative situation thus predominates, although an authorial situation seems to be superimposed upon the figural, with the result that the author can resort to the authorial situation whenever necessary for presentational reasons. As a rule, however, the figural situation remains the decisive factor for the reader's imagination.

In expositional sections authorial narration is unquestionably more economical than figural or neutral presentation. For this reason it is understandable that the only lengthy passage in *The Ambassadors* where the narrative departs from the point of view and the now-and-here of the figural medium, Lambert Strether, is to be found in the first pages of the work. Strether has just arrived in Chester; shortly before he had met Maria Gostrey, to whom is assigned the role of Strether's most important confidante. Strether and Maria Gostrey have decided to take a walk through the town together. Maria Gostrey is already awaiting him as he, coming from his room, approaches her. At this moment the reader, who has until this point perceived the fictional world through the eyes of Strether, directs his attention to Strether's outward appearance. Were *The Amassadors* a first-person novel, this moment would have taken place immediately beforehand. Strether would have mustered himself in the mirror before having to expose himself to the critical eyes of Maria Gostrey. This is the only place in the entire novel where the reader is permitted to view Strether from without. The standpoint of observation seems to lie for a moment with Maria Gostrey, but the narrator hesitates in actually surrendering the point of view to her: "When, in a quarter of an hour, he came down, what his hostess saw, what she might have taken in with a vision kindly adjusted, was the lean, slightly loose figure of a man of middle height. . . ." Immediately following these lines the narrative situation becomes unequivocally authorial as the narrator brings into play his own spatio-temporal orientation rather than that of Strether:

> [Strether] stopped on the grass, before reaching her, and went through the form of feeling for something, possibly forgotten, in the light overcoat he carried on his arm; yet the essence of the act was no more than the impulse to gain time. Nothing could have been more odd than Strether's feeling, at that moment, that he was launched in something of which the sense would be quite disconnected from the sense of his past, and which was literally beginning there and then. (p. 7)

The demonstrative in "at that moment," which indicates temporal distance between the event and the act of narration, and the "there and then" spoken from the point of view of the narrator in place of Strether's "here and now" make it clear that the center of orientation lies not in Strether but in the now-and-here of the narrator. Following this passage, however, the temporal adverb "now" is employed almost exclusively for the present time of Strether's experiences—a technique which conforms to the orientation of the figural novel.

Except for these departures which tend toward the authorial form, the novel is figural. The presentational point of view is assigned to Strether throughout. Strether, to be sure, reflects upon his experiences, but since he neither reports them himself, nor becomes aware of his self-presentation, he is an authentic figural medium with the same passive relationship to the presentation as a mirror holding the image of an object. Since Strether remains passive and the narrator prefers to stay in the background, scenic presentation becomes the predominant mode of narration. An obvious further consequence of this technique is the large number and the length of the dialogues. This extensive dialogization of the narrative is achieved by the abundant use of confidantes or "ficelles," as James calls them, employing an expression of the French stage. Thus, in her lengthy conversations with Strether Maria Gostrey, "the most unmitigated and abandoned of *ficelles*,"[12] largely assumes the customary task of the authorial narrator—the unfolding of the past in its most important elements up to the present time of the characters. It is also evident from the "Preface" that Henry James intended above all, with the help of these "ficelles," to avoid the necessity of resorting to an authorial narrative situation. He introduced them, he said, "to wave away with energy the custom of the seated mass of explanation after the fact, the inserted block of merely referential narrative."[13] "The whole lumpish question of Strether's 'past' "[14] is treated in a manner quite close to that of the analytic drama.

Approximately the same amount of space as the dialogues is occupied by the presentation of Strether's thoughts, moods, and perceptions. The next to the last chapter, a general elucidation of the possibilities for the presentation of consciousness, will continue this discussion of the stylistic techniques for presenting the processes of consciousness. Here suffice it to say that in the sections where consciousness is presented Strether's point of view always determines the field of observation and that the figural narrative situation is maintained throughout.

Although authorial elements are occasionally evident in *The Ambassadors* the novel was nevertheless conceived and written as a figural novel. The proof for this is not only to be found in the *Notebooks* and the scenario. It can also be demonstrated for those levels of the narrative which, in general, were not subject to the conscious control of the author during the course of composition and which therefore directly reveal the narrative disposition of the author. These levels must now be investigated more precisely.

A conspicuous characteristic of authorial narration is the compression of the stream of events by means of the narrative report. The author is capable of increasing or decreasing the tempo of the narrative by compressing the narrated material to varying degrees. Severe compression is only possible in the authorial report—including, of course, reports interpolated by novel figures themselves. For this reason any severely compressive type of presentation in a third-person novel will sooner or later produce an authorial narrative situation in the mind of the reader. In the figural novel such compressive reports will be avoided in general or they will be worked into the course of the action itself with the aid of confidant roles. For the same reason the figural novel will contain a time structure totally different from that of the authorial novel. Since the authorial novel tends by nature to present portions of the story in a high degree of compression its narrated time extends as a rule over incomparably greater spans of time than the narrated time of the figural novel, where compression can be achieved only indirectly. Philip Toynbee's *Tea with Mrs. Goodman*[15] encompasses both a narrative time and a narrated time approximately as long as a tea party.

The author of a figural novel need not always choose such a narrowly bounded story. An active time span which is presented in a low degree of compression and with a predominantly scenic technique can be extended, in the consciousness of a character, deep into the past. Virginia Woolf portrays in *Mrs. Dalloway* just a few hours in the course of a given day. During these hours the thoughts of several of the characters reach back into the past, so that the reader by the end of the novel has learned the fates of these characters not only on this one day, but also in broad outline during their entire lives.

The narrated time of *The Ambassadors* lasts from the beginning of the spring when Strether arrives in Paris until approximately the middle of the following summer. Even this limited time span of less than a half year still requires rather large leaps in presentation. These leaps lie almost exclusively between the individual chapters and the corresponding narrated time. When it is necessary to bridge a large span of time in the middle of a chapter (since the novel appeared first in installments, James did not always have a completely free hand with regard to chapter divisions) this takes place as a rule by means of retrospection on the part of Strether from a point beyond the intervening time span. Occasionally such retrospection is only attributed to Strether after the fact, as in the following remark:

"These, however, were but parenthetic memories [of Strether]" (p. 120). One could conceive of these as originally authorial passages which were later adjusted to the figural narrative situation.

The intervening stretches of time and those presented in severe compression also contribute to the reader's image of the fictional world, although quite differently from the actualized, fully realized time phases. The passages in which a narrative unit, especially a chapter, begins and concludes become the decisive factor for the realization of these intervening time phases in the reader's mind. This is because in the mind of the reader narrated time cannot tolerate "discontinuities" any more readily than can real time. In literary presentation, however, "flowing continuity" is only the exception, and this only for short stretches of narration. Even when there is outward correspondence between narrated time and narrative time, in other words between the elapsed time of action and the elapsed time of reading, the depth and density of every individual moment of experienced reality are necessarily reduced to the monodimensionality of their literary transmission. This depth and density of the individual moment of experience can attain approximate realization only by the overexpansion of narrative time—a technique, however, of which the author can make only sparing use. As a rule, the mind of the reader requires by no means such an exhaustive presentation in order to create the effect of a flowing continuity of narration. Time gaps which arise of necessity in the course of presentation are filled by the tacit transference of the quality, the mood, and the symbolic values of the realized time phases into the empty phases. Thus the empty, indefinite, or dead stretches of time attain "qualitative coloring." Roman Ingarden holds that although such "empty" or merely secondary time phases do not have a fixed content, a qualitative coloring "of some sort could be intended"[16] for them all the same. Robert Petsch has coined the term "empty" or "dead" stretches of narration. He, too, has found evidence for indirect qualitative characterization of these stretches of time: "In this period [i.e. the empty stretch of time] something grew, and even the most faintly . . . marked passage of time is itself a symbol of this growth. It also maintains the tensional level of the narrative and hence our epic attitude, our anticipation of further developments."[17] The division of a novel into chapters, paragraphs, etc. thus not only serves an outer ordering function, but also has great significance for the novel's inner structure of meaning. It emphasizes the places where the presentation of densely realized time shifts to the empty time of the intervening or compressed stretches and where the narrative shifts back from empty time to a realized time phase. At these points one must seek those references, signals, and symbols which give the mind of the reader an indication of the type of qualitative coloring which should fill the empty time phases.

In examining the chapter endings in *The Ambassadors* one must keep in mind that in a figural novel the chapter endings must usually be formed without authorial assistance. Summaries, prefigurations, transitions, which all serve to color the subsequent empty stretch of time to some degree, cannot be employed. For this reason most of the chapters in *The Ambassadors* end in the middle of a dialogue. Only occasionally does this interruption of the scene correspond to the end of a phase in the external action, for example, the exit of someone who had taken part in the conversation. Often a single sentence is thrust out to the very edge of the realized time phase, to the point where the empty phase begins. In this position an especially strong emphasis falls on individual words. Such emphasis often gives the final words a certain symbolic power or a pointed, epigrammatic tone which then acts as a motto or leitmotif for the subsequent empty stretch of time. Other chapters end with the presentation of Strether's reflections. They show Strether as if on the threshold of a new insight into his situation and into the complex relationships of his surrounding world. The subsequent empty stretch of time then serves to indicate the process by which Strether finally thinks through the new situation and makes his deductions from it. Strether quits the scene with furrowed brow, only to enter again in the next chapter with a new insight and often in a different position as a result. Only in a very few chapters does the author-narrator let himself be heard, in order personally to bring the scene to a close. Aside from these few cases of authorial chapter endings, the empty stretches between the chapters are anticipated and given qualitative coloring within the limits and possibilities of the figural narrative situation.

In *The Ambassadors* the beginnings of chapters and narrative sections also lack the usual narrative preliminaries. It is not always possible, however, to employ a pure scenic start, that is, to open the scene with an action or conversation already in progress. The narrative context often makes it necessary to recapitulate at least the main points of the action or development during the preceding empty phase. In such a case the principle of narrative economy precludes using scenic presentation for every one of these events. In *The Ambassadors* retrospection by the main figure is the usual means of recapitulating the intervening stretch of the action. A large number of chapters begin with the verb in the past-perfect tense. The narrative situation of the figural novel causes the experiential present of the figural medium to become the imaginative present of the reader; the epic preterite takes on the imaginative value of the present. Thus the retrospective past-perfect has the imaginative value of the simple past. The beginning of the tenth chapter is perhaps the best example of this. The first sentence contains a time designation—somewhat authorial in tone—which establishes the intended experiential present of the main figure. The past perfect of the second verb can already be viewed from the experiential present of Strether: "The Sunday of the next week was a wonderful day, and Chad Newsome had let his friend know in advance that he had provided for it. There had already been a question of his taking him to see the great Gloriani . . ." (p. 133). It subsequently becomes clear that this flashback represents a retrospection on the part of Strether. It takes place at the moment of his arrival at the home of an artist in the Faubourg

Saint-Germain, where he had been invited for an afternoon gathering. From the very first the experiential present of Strether, the now-and-here of the figural medium, and thus the reader's center of orientation all lie in this moment of Strether's arrival at the home of Gloriani, even though there is no reference to this point in the narrative. The past-perfect tense, however, gives rise to the expectation that the temporal zero-point must be located sometime during that Sunday. This must be the experiential present from which the past is experienced in the form of the retrospective past perfect. On Strether's arrival, or as soon as he has "found himself" there, the past perfect gives way to the simple preterite. This shift establishes the spot where the now-and-here of the figural medium lay all along; it is the spot to which the reader's center of orientation was being drawn. At the beginning of the following passage Strether is already at Gloriani's house, but he is still occupied with the pre-history of this visit:

> The most he had, at all events, asked of his companion was whether the persons in question were French; and that inquiry had been but a proper comment on the sound of their name. "Yes. That is no!" had been Chad's reply; but he had immediately added that their English was the most charming in the world, so that if Strether were wanting an excuse for not getting on with them he wouldn't in the least find one. Never in fact had Strether —in the mood into which the place had quickly launched him— felt, for himself, less the need of an excuse. . . . His fellow-guests were multiplying. . . . The place itself was a great impression—a small pavilion, clearfaced and sequestered. . . . (p. 134)

The first occurrence which reaches directly into Strether's experiential present is indicated by the verb in "never in fact had Strether . . . felt;" the verb, to be sure, is in the past perfect, but it is a case of present perfect shifted into the epic past.

According to a convention of the figural novel the bearer of consciousness or the figural medium reveals the processes of his consciousness as an object, in the third person. This does not mean that in the reader's imagination the author must always appear as the corresponding subject. In the case of true figural mediation the reader sees himself as the subject. The first part of the above passage represents retrospection of the novel's central figure; it is not simply an authorial report used to recapitulate previous events. This is clear from the tense employed to present the reflections, thoughts, or feelings which Strether associates with the retrospective view of the events. Even in the context of retrospection these thoughts and emotions are presented in the epic preterite, for they belong to Strether's experiential present at the moment of retrospection. The sentence just prior to this passage will illustrate: "Did he wish to spring them, in the Woollett phrase, with a fuller force—to confound his critic, slight though as yet the criticism, with some form of merit exquisitely incalculable?"

Strether has come to Paris with a special mission. He is supposed to free Chad, whose mother is the widow of a New England industrialist, from the ties of a supposed liaison in Paris. He is to bring Chad back to New England to take over the family business. As a reward for Strether there is the chance of a marriage with Mrs. Newsome, Chad's mother. Only gradually does Chad learn the background of Strether's mission. One day there is an open confrontation between the two. The eighth chapter begins in the middle of the conversation. Sections of the conversation which took place before the beginning of the chapter are again given by a kind of retrospective on the part of Strether. The following sentence clearly shows that the flashback represents Strether's reviewal: " 'Do I strike you as improved?' Strether was to recall that Chad had at this point inquired" (p. 102). One has the impression that at a critical point in the conversation Strether lets what has been said pass once more before his mind's eye before speaking the final word. And in fact, the transition in narrated time from the past perfect to the preterite reveals that this critical point is the moment when Chad actually forces Strether to admit the real reasons for his journey:

> "Your engagement to my mother has become then what they call here a *fait accompli*?"—it had consisted, the determinant touch, in nothing more than that.
> Well, that was enough, Strether had felt while his answer hung

fire. He had felt at the same time, however, that nothing could less become him than that it should hang fire too long. "Yes," he said brightly, "it was on the happy settlement of the question that I started. You see therefore to what tune I'm in your family. Moreover," he added, "I've been supposing you'd suppose it."

(p. 103)

From this point on the conversation is presented as present action in the preterite; the reader seems to be a third person, listening to the two. This retrospective recapitulation of the beginning of the conversation makes it possible to avoid the use of extensive direct discourse and to present Strether's memory of what was said in a suitably abbreviated form. At first the reader does not direct his attention to the individual words of the conversation, only to encounter the speakers in a sudden dramatic confrontation at the moment when the decisive words are spoken.

The typical beginning of a narrative section in *The Ambassadors* is characterized in the following way. Strether's experiential present and thus the reader's center of orientation are projected forward to a significant point in the action. At this point a critical event stimulates Strether to renewed reflection which leads to a retrospective view of the immediate past.

In one respect the scenic presentation of the action in the figural novel is of greater importance for the reader's imagination than the reportlike presentation of an event in the authorial novel. In the latter case the reader's center of orientation lies in the narrative act. The narrated material is understood as a report, as a compressive summary which is presented across the narrative distance from a secure point in time. In the figural novel, on the other hand, the action takes place before the eyes of the reader, like a dramatic event on stage. The center of orientation lies in the scene and seems to shift with the course of the fictional event.

It is therefore necessary to investigate how this shift in the center of orientation is accomplished. This question deserves special attention because of the effect on the imagination of the reader. It was established above that the literary image in words can never attain a state of flowing continuity. Yet in scenic presentation the reader's imagination seems, according to all experience, to apprehend the fictional action as a continuous course of events. The image in words and the reader's image are not fully congruous. This discrepancy is least noticeable in a full dialogue scene. Here the novel comes closest to dramatic presentation on the stage, although the literary dialogue scene itself is not completely monodimensional. One must take into account the speaking characters' exteriors, their mannerisms and gestures. The reader, who knows all these aspects of the characters from earlier passages in the novel, will apprehend them along with his image of the dialogue scene. In this way he is able to incorporate the action between the words—the accompanying gestures and expressions—into his mental image even though they are not really presented in the dialogue scene. Here the reader's constant desire to achieve coexistence in the fictional material serves to create continuity. This creative element is able to give qualitative coloring to the temporal holes which gape between the words and sentences of a dialogue in its literary presentation.

The written image and the mental image differ even more greatly in respect to continuity of action when an event is presented by means other than dialogue. The potential of language in this area must still be explored. Compare the difference in the temporal imaginative value which can be expressed by the perfective and imperfective aspects of the German verbs *erfassen* (to lay hold of, grasp) and *fassen* (to hold).

Finally the rendering of consciousness must also be noted here, since it is often presented in a style which is not analogous to speech. The presentation of the processes of consciousness can extend over many pages of a novel. Since such processes actually have no empirical temporal duration, the author can either present them within the temporal course of the narrated material or he can present them as if they possessed no temporal dimension. A typical case of processes of consciousness which are presented with no apparent narrated time has been noted in a study of the temporal structure of William Faulkner's *The Bear*.[18]

In order to discuss the question of temporal continuity it is necessary to quote a relatively long passage from *The Ambassadors*:

> "She's the most charming young girl I've ever seen. Therefore don't touch her. Don't know—don't want to know. And moreover—yes—you *won't*."
>
> It was an appeal, of a sudden, and she took it in. "As a favor to you?"
>
> "Well—since you ask me."
>
> "Anything, everything you ask," she smiled. "I sha'n't know then—never. Thank you," she added with peculiar gentleness as she turned away.
>
> The sound of it lingered with him, making him fairly feel as if he had been tripped up and had a fall. In the very act of arranging with her for his independence he had, under pressure from a particular perception, inconsistently, quite stupidly, committed himself, and, with her subtlety sensitive, on the spot, to an advantage, she had driven in, by a single word, a little golden nail, the sharp intention of which he signally felt. He had not detached, he had more closely connected himself, and his eyes, as he considered, with some intensity, this circumstance, met another pair which had just come within their range and which struck him as reflecting his sense of what he had done. He recognized them at the same moment as those of Little Bilham, who had apparently drawn near on purpose to speak to him, and Little Bilham was not, in the conditions, the person to whom his heart would be most closed. They were seated together, a minute later, at the angle of the room obliquely opposite the corner in which Gloriani was still engaged with Jeanne de Vionnet, to whom, at first, and in silence, their attention had been benevolently given. "I can't see for my life," Strether had then observed, "how a young fellow of any spirit—such a one as you, for instance—can be admitted to the sight of that young lady without being hard hit. Why don't you go in, Little Bilham?" He remembered the tone into which he had been betrayed on the garden-bench at the sculptor's reception, and this might make up for that by being much more the right sort of thing to say to a young man worthy of any advice at all. "There *would* be some reason."

"Some reason for what?"

"Why, for hanging on here."

"To offer my hand and fortune to Mlle. de Vionnet?"

"Well," Strether asked, "to what lovelier apparition *could* you offer them? She's the sweetest little thing I've ever seen."

(pp. 192–93)

This portion of a scene encompasses the end of one phase of the action and the beginning of a new phase. The end of the first phase is indicated by Mme. de Vionnet's departure, which concludes the conversation between her and Strether. The second phase begins with the entrance of Little Bilham. Between the two, as a narrative connecting link, comes a presentation of Strether's thoughts. Here, as everywhere in the novel, Strether must be regarded as the center of observation for the whole scene. In the dialogue at the beginning of the passage the present time of the action shifts along with the center of orientation— parallel to the course of the conversation. Obviously the conversation is not flowing very rapidly. The delicate subject, reflections, observation of the effect of one's words on the interlocutor, self-interruptions in the middle of a sentence—all this obstructs the flow of the words. One is struck by the number of dashes on the page. Strether twice makes a short comment or observation to himself which barely lasts long enough to occupy a normal conversational pause. In the next paragraph ("The sound of it . . .") the connecting link begins between the two phases of the external action. At the beginning of this intervening section no external action is presented; in contrast to the dialogue there is no way to measure the duration of what is presented. The processes indicated by the words "lingered" and "feel," however, do receive a perceivable temporal dimension by means of the material evoked retrospectively in Strether's consciousness during this time. The reader has the tendency simply to measure thoughts and processes of consciousness with the yardstick of the narrative time required to present them. This tendency also gives such processes the appearance of real duration. While the duration of the verb "considered" seems to be determined in the same way, the following verbs "met," "struck," and "recognized" express momentary actions which have no analogous duration. The three verbs describe three aspects in the experience of a single event. The simultaneous aspects are transposed to consecutive presentation. This, in turn, can correspond to a simultaneous realization in the reader's imagination, where what is apprehended consecutively is concentrated back into the intensity of the original experience. Another reflection of Strether follows; it appears to fill in the time between the two phases of action. With the beginning of the next sentence ("They were seated together, a minute later . . .") the narrated time leaps forward with a jerk, only to linger there for a few moments while the intervening material is retrieved as a part of Strether's consciousness. This is a repetition of the technique frequently used by James at the beginning of a chapter, where the experiential present of the figural medium is projected forward in time. The figural medium acts like the pupil of an eye: according to the degree of participation in the surrounding events it opens wide or falls half-shut. When it is half-shut certain events are automatically registered and then held ready for the moment when a fully perceived event connects with them and causes them to be concretized. With the return to dialogue, which here, too, begins with a recapitulation from Strether's consciousness, the presentation of time regains its continuous and measurable flow. The reader's center of orientation, which several times had been projected forward in spurts, smoothly follows the course of the action once again.

This passage showed that even in an apparently unified scene the time of action is not always presented in an uninterrupted and continuous flow. Although strictly speaking the reader's center of orientation must follow this uneven forward movement of the time of action, it is possible for the reader to concretize in his imagination an even and continuous flow of action. In this case it is mainly the contents of the main figure's consciousness which serve as "filler." Since the reader's imagination succeeds in compensating for the schematization of the flow of action, the reader does not become aware of the literary process. The illusion of direct presentation of the action is retained. Here, too, the novel sustains the figural narrative situation.

The question of "flowing continuity" can also be approached from another direction. A mathematically constant flow of time is basically foreign to the reader's experience, for he really knows only his own "subjective time," which differs from the point-for-point, linear arrangement of physical-mathematical time.[19] The uneven, discontinuous flow of fictional time can thus also be understood as an analogue to the unevenness and heterogeneity of this subjective time. In both cases the unevenness remains below the threshold of conscious experience.

In *The Ambassadors* not only the basic structural framework conforms to the narrative situation of the figural novel. Even in the levels of presentation which are normally beyond the author's conscious control, figural narrative conventions predominate. This leads one to believe that the narrative stance which corresponds to the figural form was already inherent in the author's original conception. As the *Notebooks* and a number of James's other works show, the theme complex of the novel had occupied the author's attention long before the actual writing of *The Ambassadors*. The first clear indication of a narrative stance which the author unconsciously assumed in treating this material can be found in an entry in the *Notebooks* with the date "Torquay, October 31st, 1895." This was approximately five years before James began to write *The Ambassadors*. On this day James makes note of an episode which a friend had reported to him. An elderly author addresses the following words to a younger friend:

"Oh, you are young, you are young—be glad of it: be glad of it and *live*. Live all you can: it's a mistake not to. It doesn't so much matter what you do—but live. This place makes it all come over me. I see it now. I haven't done so—and now I'm old. It's too late. It has gone past me—I've lost it. You have time. You are young. Live!" (*Notebooks*, p. 226)

It is not difficult to see in this entry the germ of the idea of *The Ambassadors*. Especially revealing, however, is the process by which the stimulus is first assimilated. The process is visible in the entries immediately following the original one. The decisive passage reads: "I amplify and improve a little—but that was the tone. It touches me—I can see him—I can hear him. Immediately, of course—as everything, thank God, does—it suggests a little situation. I seem to see something, of a tiny kind, springing out of it . . ." (*Notebooks*, p. 226). This vivid realization of a scene which the author has already adopted into a novelistic plot may not be unusual. Here it is characteristic of an attitude which the author retained through the entire writing of the novel.

At the very beginning of the scenario, which James wrote for *The Ambassadors* five years after these entries as a kind of synopsis for his publisher, one can observe the same stance of the author. He stands directly opposite the events, as if they were present before him. Strether is now presented as "an American, of the present hour," the whole work is called "The picture [sic] of a certain momentous and interesting period."[20] The intense creation of presentness in the material changes the author into a stage manager who sends the figures he has conceived onto an imaginary stage, while he himself gives introductory commentary. In accordance with this role he also speaks in the present tense rather than in the preterite, which is the narrative tense of a "reporting" author. "Waymark is an overworked lawyer in an American business community. . . . After a little, however, Chad comes on the scene."[21]

In places the scenario already takes the from of dialogue. Here the impression of a procession of characters on the stage, improvised by the author acting as stage manager, is strengthened by the present tense of the *verba dicendi*:

> "Oh, I see what you're thinking—that Paris is an awful place, and that it may be awfully difficult. But it will be all the more fun."
> "Fun?" poor Strether rather ruefully echoes.
> "It's just the sort of job," she replies, "that's really, I assure you, in my line and that I should be quite ready to hand in an estimate for. Upon my word, I'd take the order."

"I wish to goodness then you would!" her companion laughs.
"It would save me a lot of trouble!" (*Notebooks*, p. 386)

Although the presentational tense in the scenario is already the present tense, this tense makes an especially strong impression in the *verba dicendi* of this dialogue. The author dramatizes, activates the scene from his conception of the work, and at the same time he foregoes every narrative guise. In conjunction with the perceivable presence of the author (as narrator) a preterite form would immediately remove the figures a temporal step away from the author's narrative present.

An analogy to this use of the present tense can, of course, also be found in the so-called reproductive present used in giving the contents of a literary work or retelling it. The present is preferred to the epic preterite of the literary version because the present transmits the original experience of reading the work, the immediate image of the course of events. In this situation the epic preterite would cause the listener to focus on the fact that everything is being narrated, that is, being reported. The reproductive present tense can thus be seen as an expression of the reader's imaginative experience during the process of reading. What is experienced and presented as present is here expressed by the present tense, since the original narrative process need not be separated temporally from the narrated action. For the same reason the retelling (in brief) of an authorial novel will be done in the reproductive present if the temporal distance between the narrator and the narrated action can be disregarded. If the present tense is used for the retelling, however, only the present tense will be available for both temporal levels—that of the narrated action and that of the narrative act. The following hypothetical sentence illustrates this: "In Part Five of *The Ambassadors* James describes the scene in which Strether addresses the following words to Little Bilham. . . ." The process of levelling a work's various time terraces also accounts for the difficulties which often arise in the present-tense retelling of multiple-frame narratives.

This interpretation of the reproductive present tense can also be applied to the scenario of *The Ambassadors*. In the scenario, however, it is not a case of retelling, but rather of "pretelling," since the novel had not yet been written and had no existence outside the author's conception. This pretelling or preview still lacks the process of stylizing into reportlike narration what is past and completed—a stylistic process which is accomplished by every real narrative. For this reason the present tense in the scenario has the same meaning for James as the reproductive present tense of a retelling has for the reteller. The tense causes what is pretold to appear as the author's present imaginative process. If James imagined as present each scene of the action both in the scenario and earlier in the notation of his first flashes of inspiration, it is reasonable to suppose that this original narrative stance reappeared in the final composition of the novel. It should be added, however, that despite this conceptional tendency to create presentness James could also have directed his novel toward an authorial narrative situation. The structure of meaning of such a novel, to be sure, would have been fundamentally different from that of *The Ambassadors*.

One final point must still be considered. In his pretelling of the novel the author uses the present tense to express his vision of the action *in actu*. In his retelling of the novel the reader narrates in the present tense in accord with his *in actu* imagination of the action. Between these two present imaginative experiences of the action stands the novel itself, in which the action is expressed by the form of the epic preterite. The author's *in actu* vision can flow into the form of the epic preterite; this epic preterite can in turn evoke the effect of presentness in the reader's imagination; under these conditions the epic preterite has the imaginative value of the present. In an authorial narrative situation, on the other hand, the narrative distance between the act of narration and the action puts special emphasis on the "beforehand" aspect indicated by the epic preterite. What is narrated in the preterite is understood as something past. It has been established that the temporal step from the narrative act to the action is not expressed in a pretelling or a retelling. This means that the authorial narrative situation of a novel only attains the possibility of adequate expression in the epic preterite. In the composition of the final version of the novel the designation of the temporal step between the narrative act and the action becomes a part of the presentation of the action. Since the reteller strives to simplify the narrative by including only the main action it is understandable that he simply leaves out the designation of the narrative act and the temporal step which separates this act from the time level of the action.

These relationships indicate the demands which are made of the epic preterite as a narrative tense. The epic tense must be capable of expressing the temporal step from the "afterwards" of the narrative act to the "beforehand" of the action. The "beforehand" temporal relationship finds adequate designation in the past-time meaning of the preterite. When the narrative situation causes the presented material to appear as present, however, the "beforehand" quality of the epic preterite is not realized in the reader's imagination. In a figural novel the transformation of the narration of an action into the epic preterite thus forms a part of the stylization process to which reality is subjected in literary presentation. Just as the uneven, discontinuous presentation of a course of action regains its original, flowing continuity in the reader's imagination, the reader is also able, in the proper narrative situation, to transpose the imaginative value of the epic preterite into the present.

The use of the present tense as a narrative tense should also be seen in this context. Again and again attempts are made to compose entire novels in the present tense rather than in the epic preterite. These attempts can be viewed as further evidence of the fact that under certain conditions the reader imagines a narrated event as occurring in the present. Authors who have elevated the present to a narrative tense believe that they are giving special consideration to an imaginative tendency of the reader. In reality this technique does not always succeed in doing the reader a service. It is clear from the previous discussion of orientation in the novel that for the realization of the narrative distance an authorial narrative situation requires the temporal dimension which is attained by employing the epic preterite to designate the present time of action. In the figural novel, where the narrative distance is not designated, it will as a rule be easier to employ the present tense as the narrative tense. This can be illustrated by two novels which are written in the present tense. Franz Werfel's *Das Lied von Bernadette* contains numerous passages with a distinct authorial narrative situation (e.g. the beginning of Chapter 32). In these passages the present tense is the narrative tense; it causes a certain uneasiness, for one cannot always distinguish the statement of general truths from the presentation of the specific event. Moreover, the narrator and the narrative act are forced into apparent simultaneity with the narrated events. Such simultaneity is as inappropriate to this novel's narrative mode—with occasional high compression and frequent leaps in the plot—as it is to the quality of superior insight now and then exhibited by the narrator. Joyce Cary's *Mister Johnson* avoids the authorial narrative situation in general and limits itself for the most part to scenic presentation of a very simple course of events. Here the choice of the present as narrative tense seems more fortunate than in Werfel's novel.

The figural novel must still be assigned its theoretical place. In the discussion of the first-person novel the point was already found at which a first-person novel (without designation of the narrative act) becomes a figural novel if the first-person form is simply changed to a third-person form. *The Ambassadors* should be pinpointed a short distance away from this point, which represents the extreme use of the figural narrative situation. The clearer the authorial elements in a figural novel—above all the designation of the narrator's presence—the closer this novel will come to the typological point of the authorial novel. For this reason the figural narrative situation is linked on the one hand to the first-person novel (without designation of the narrative act), and on the other hand to the authorial novel. In this way the theoretical place where all novel types can be sought according to their narrative situations can be viewed as a circle. The conclusions which can be drawn from this closed pattern will be treated further in the last chapter.

V

ULYSSES

THE NOVELS INVESTIGATED thus far presented no difficulties in establishing the place of the various novel types in relation
to the genre in general. The reason for their obvious theoretical
positions can be found in the unity of the narrative situation
employed. All these novels give the reader an assurance on the
very first page, so to speak, that the initial guise of the mediative
process—authorial or first-person—will be retained throughout
the entire work. Where departure from this guise becomes un-
avoidable a corresponding explanation must be given for it in the
narrative.

If any of the common classifications of James Joyce's *Ulysses*[1]
were really adequate (such as the following by C. H. Rickwood:
"Nothing in *Ulysses* is, to use Mr. Lubbock's distinction, reported;
everything is shown or dramatized"[2]) then *Ulysses* would simply
be a consistent figural novel. As even a superficial examination of
the novel shows, however, predominantly figural parts stand
beside distinctly authorial sections; at least two chapters, moreover, are rendered in the first-person form. Although the unity of
narrative situation is thus violated in *Ulysses*, prognoses to the
effect that with *Ulysses* the form of the novel must be regarded
as outmoded—even T. S. Eliot voiced this opinion when the
novel appeared[3]—are untenable. The following analysis will show

that in *Ulysses* only a few traditional narrative conventions were suspended; the most important among these is the convention which demands unity of narrative situation. At the same time *Ulysses* introduced new narrative forms, some of which have already made their way into the general stock of conventions. Still others, one may assume, will do the same in the future.

The majority of guises taken by the authorial and the first-person narrative situation vary the archtypal epic situation, in which a personal narrator tells something to a group of listeners. Joyce, too, employs narrative guises in *Ulysses* which are derived from this basic situation, but the parodistic intention in every individual case is unmistakable. In its totality *Ulysses* is no longer affected by considerations derived from this archtypal narrative situation. Joyce accepts the fact that in the novel there is no longer any "narrating" but only reading, that is, seeing what is printed. He concludes that in writing a novel the novelist can overlook the traditional conventions of "narrating," and can just as well attend to the conditions which arise from the fact that he only reaches his reader by means of the printed page. The possibilities of formation, structure, and expression which are contained in the printed page have thus determined the structure of *Ulysses* to a high degree. In his own way Sterne made extensive use of these possibilities long before Joyce.

It is important to note, however, that this exploitation of the visual aspects of the printed novel determines above all the work's total structure and the external form of individual chapters. Due to the verbal-stylistic level of the novel many passages actually require oral presentation, for only in this way can all the text's sound associations and the rhythmic structure of the sentences be realized.

In this manner Joyce can borrow structural forms from areas which have rarely influenced the form of literary presentation. Above all he attempts to make use of subliterary models, such as the newspaper and the catechism. Joyce also borrows structural forms for his novel from the other arts, particularly from music.

Ulysses begins as a figural novel. Stephen Dedalus is the figural medium through which the reader views the fictional world. Yet behind this figural medium—as in *The Ambassadors*—stands the author, who intrudes above all during the presentation of external events. In the second and third chapters ("Nestor—The School," "Proteus—The Strand") the presentation limits itself more and more to Stephen's point of view. Only in the fourth chapter, in which Leopold Bloom appears for the first time ("Calypso—The House") does the authorial element begin to emerge again more strongly, for here the task is to introduce Bloom. A change in the figural medium takes place in this chapter. Here the presentation begins to follow Bloom. In the next two chapters ("Lotus-eaters —The Bath," "Hades—The Graveyard") the authorial element withdraws somewhat, since Bloom is sufficiently established, as it were, as the figural medium.

Until this point a figural medium is always present on the scene; the presentation simply sketched the picture of its impressions and thoughts. In the chapter "Hades—The Graveyard" for the first time a short course of events is presented which is not registered by the figural medium (pp. 100 and 104–05). In the next chapter, "Aeolus—The Newspaper," the point of view is transferred from Bloom back again to Stephen. Here, too, between Bloom's surrender of the point of view and Stephen's reacceptance of it occurs a short scenic passage which is not assigned to any of the figures (pp. 128–30). This is a departure from the narrative convention of the figural novel; convention requires the continuous presence of a "central intelligence," as James calls it. At the same time, however, no distinct authorial tone of narration can be perceived.

The segmentation which is characteristic of the entire work also appears in the newspaper chapter. By using this technique of presentation Joyce departs from the conventions of "narrating." The presentation of the action is interrupted by titles in the manner of newspaper headlines; it is subdivided into segments which move the action forward, though without regard for the external segmentation. The insertion of these headlines is an attempt to use the printed page of the novel to augment the work's presentational capacity. The appearance of such a page imitates to a certain extent the appearance of a newspaper. At the same time the fragmentary, catchwordlike quality of journalistic news presentation is parodied. In this respect the headlines represent the first of many stylistic parodies in *Ulysses*. Stylistic parody here parallels the fictional events at the newspaper by commenting on these events, though in an ironic, distanced manner. The "headlines" are arranged so as to mirror the development from the dignified style of Victorian newspapers to the vulgar "slickness of the modern press."[4] The stylistic parodies are similarly arranged in the "Oxen of the Sun" chapter, "The Hospital." There they mirror simultaneously the development of the embryo and the development of human speech. The next two chapters continue the novel's initial, predominantly figural narrative situation with minor variations. In the chapter "Lestrygonians—The Lunch" Bloom is once again the figural medium. The following episode, "Scylla and Charybdis—The Library," is mirrored in Stephen's consciousness. Thus the first nine chapters (from the beginning to "Scylla and Charybdis") manifest approximately the same type of narrative situation—figural presentation through the consciousness of one of the two main characters with occasional authorial additions.

Up to this point the novel proceeds with relatively traditional treatment of structure and narrative situation (the chapter "Aeolus—The Newspaper" is an exception); in the next chapter, "Wandering Rocks—The Streets," the large-scale literary experiment begins. During a period of approximately a half-hour the main figures and a number of secondary figures are shown on their various wanderings throughout the city. Each figure is assigned a chapter segment in which a stretch of journey is presented. A complex of word-motifs, as well as numerous meetings among the individual figures, demonstrates the coexistence of all these brief scenes. At least once, moreover, every figure is brought into contact with Father Conmee's journey through the city and with the viceregal cavalcade. The complex of coincidence and fate, intention and meaninglessness, in these people's paths is revealed only to the reader who can survey all these figures in their individual states. The figures themselves wander blindly between the walls of the buildings, each alone, like the symbolic blind man who gropes his way with his cane through the streets.

This is the first consistent use of the technique of segmentation, which then becomes the basic structural principle of most of the subsequent chapters. Segmentation is a part of Joyce's new presentational situation. Since there is no longer any "narrating," the customary preliminaries at the beginning and end of a narrative section are omitted; there is nothing to facilitate the reader's transition from one part to the next. The presentation begins in the middle of a scene and ends just as abruptly, only to take up another thread of the plot *in medias res*. This mode of presentation also does away with all authorial interpretation and commentary. This segmentation, however, has one characteristic which serves in part to explain the frequency of its use in *Ulysses*. Because these brief scenes are strung out without commentary or transition they come into contrast with one another. Such contrasts can give rise to almost every conceivable interpretative effect, such as tragedy, comedy, irony, pathos, satire, parody, according to the expressive intention of the author. In this way the fictional material undergoes interpretation by the author even though he never reveals himself in a single word. Authorial commentary is replaced by a process of rearrangement in which the fictional material interprets itself. The author's personal intrusion, which always takes place by narration—that is, by the words and voice of the authorial narrator—is now abstracted, depersonalized; it attains visible form in the geometry of the novel's structure.

The author's withdrawal to such a position only became possible after the surrender of the traditional narrative stance, which still evoked the image of the oral narrator's presence. Segmentation is thus a structural technique which corresponds above all to the presentational situation of the author as writer and editor of the printed page. The question of the author's now-and-here in such a segmented passage is meaningless. The reader's center of orientation lies in the scenic moment of action. By means of the difference between the novel's arrangement of the action and one's daily experience of reality the narrative structure serves as a constant reminder that this action has been "formed" and therefore possesses a higher degree of meaningfulness than empirical reality.

The setting of the next chapter, "Sirens—The Concert Room," is formed by the adjoining guest rooms of the Ormond Hotel. In the presentation of the events in this setting short segments are interspersed which briefly show people who at this moment are located in other parts of the city, but who are related to each other by the action. One of these people is Bloom, who himself finally comes to the Ormond. On the way he crosses Essex Bridge. At the same time Lenehan enters the bar of the hotel, where one of the two barmaids is trilling one of the year's popular operetta tunes, "Oh, My Dolores," to herself:

> Gaily Miss Douce polished a tumbler, trilling:
> —*O, Idolores, queen of the eastern seas!*
> —Was Mr Lidwell in today?
> In came Lenehan. Round him peered Lenehan. Mr Bloom reached Essex Bridge. Yes, Mr Bloom crossed bridge of Yessex. To Martha I must write. Buy paper. Daly's. Girl there civil. Bloom. Old Bloom. Blue Bloom is on the rye.
> —He was in at lunchtime, Miss Douce said.
> Lenehan came forward . . .   (p. 257)

Here the segment "Mr Bloom reached . . . on the rye" forms a thematic unit. Without being distinguished typographically from the context of the scene this segment is woven into the motif complex of the scene in the manner of a musical theme.

In the first part of this chapter the scene in the bar is not clearly observed by any one consciousness. Nevertheless, even this part of the action is presented as if it were the contents of someone's consciousness; the style indicates not an oral presentation but rather an interior monologue of the author. Direct discourse flows without any signal into indirect discourse or narrated monologue. The rendering of consciousness and the presentation of external events are extensively intermingled. Narrator's comments are completely absent. None of the figures present can clearly be regarded as the medium of presentation in the chapter. The events are mirrored in an impersonal consciousness which belongs to none of the figures. Frequently the normal idiomatic and syntactic arrangement of the words is relinquished in order to reproduce the fictional action in filmlike approximation of the duration and continuity of the flow of events. This mode of presentation is characterized by a continuous attempt to move the mimesis of reality away from the realm of the words' meanings and into the body of the word itself, into the sound and sight pattern of the language. This attempt lays claim to those very expressive capabilities of language which are generally least at home in the stylization of a narrator's report. One should also not overlook the fact that Joyce sometimes threatens to succumb to the "fallacy of imitative form."

The apparently impersonal medium of presentation appears ultimately as a bearer of consciousness; it is equipped with the capability of memory and can thus transfer ideas, motifs, and word-echoes from one segment to another segment with a completely different perspective of observation. A passage from the chapter in the Ormond Hotel, "Sirens—The Concert Room," will illustrate this. At the beginning of the quotation appear the tea-drinking, giggling barmaids, Miss Douce and Miss Kennedy. The verbal presentation attempts, as far as possible, a direct verbal reproduction of the scene. The aim is to portray the actual duration and continuity of the events behind the bar, occasionally even the simultaneity of these events. Miss Douce and Miss Kennedy have seen Bloom as he passes by the hotel and now giggle at the inconceivable prospect of marriage with this figure. At the end of the passage the presentation shifts to Bloom, who meanwhile has walked a few houses further. Now the impersonal medium of presentation gives him the appellation "Greaseabloom." Evidently this must be regarded as thought preserverance of the image group "Bloom—greasy," which had already appeared in the conversation of the two barmaids. The impersonal medium thus does not register fictional reality mechanically, like a movie camera, but brings its own consciousness into play. The presentation then takes the form of an interior monologue in which Bloom's momentary thoughts are expressed. Without any transition there is then a change in the technique of presentation and in the point of view of observation. The reader finds himself once again in the bar of the Ormond:

> Miss Kennedy lipped her cup again, raised, drank a sip and giggle-giggled. Miss Douce, bending again over the teatray, ruffled again her nose and rolled droll fattened eyes. Again Kenneygiggles, stooping her fair pinnacles of hair, stooping, her tortoise napecomb showed, spluttered out of her mouth her tea, choking in tea and laughter, coughing with choking, crying:
> —O greasy eyes! Imagine being married to a man like that, she cried. With his bit of beard!
> Douce gave full vent to a splendid yell, a full yell of full woman, delight, joy, indignation.
> —Married to the greasy nose! she yelled.
> Shrill, with deep laughter, after bronze in gold, they urged each each to peal after peal, ringing in changes, bronzegold goldbronze, shrilldeep, to laughter after laughter. And then laughed more. Greasy I knows. Exhausted, breathless their shaken heads they laid, braided and pinnacled by glossycombed, against the counterledge. All flushed (O!), panting, sweating (O!), all breathless.
> Married to Bloom, to greaseaseabloom.
> —O saints above! Miss Douce said, sighed above her jumping rose. I wished I hadn't laughed so much. I feel all wet.
> —O, Miss Douce! Miss Kennedy protested. You horrid thing!
> And flushed yet more (you horrid!), more goldenly.
> By Cantwell's offices roved Greaseabloom, by Ceppi's virgins, bright of their oils. Nannetti's father hawked those things about, wheedling at doors as I. Religion pays. Must see him about Keyes's par. Eat first. I want. Not yet. At four, she said. Time ever passing. Clockhands turning. On. Where eat? The Clarence, Dolphin. On. For Raoul. Eat. If I net five guineas with those ads. The violet silk petticoats. Not yet. The sweets of sin.
> Flushed less, still less, goldenly paled.
> Into their bar strolled Mr Dedalus. (pp. 256–57)

The medium in this passage cannot be defined by means of the categories used here. It manifests authorial and figural traits; it seems to be impersonal, neutral; at the same time, however, traces of the mirroring of consciousness can be found in the presentation. The presentation of that which is spoken and that which is thought sometimes flows together as if everything had been apprehended and refracted by a consciousness one more time. The tendency of the authorial medium to depersonalize the narrative and to distance the mode of presentation as far as possible from the customary reportlike stylization of the action is a characteristic feature of *Ulysses*.

The chapter "Sirens—The Concert Room" is preceded by a prelude in rhythmic prose. This prelude has given rise to more commentary than one might expect from its length of scarcely two pages. The reasons for the great critical interest in this passage can probably be seen in the fact that here Joyce extends his literary experiment to the outermost limit. In this prelude word-motifs appear which have been extracted from the context of the following chapter. The commentaries speak almost universally of a kind of overture to the "Sirens" chapter. The question of the meaning of these word-motifs is problematical; they seem to have been extracted indiscriminately and arranged just as indiscriminately. Ernst Robert Curtius says that "this ostensibly meaningless text . . . represents an overture: he [Joyce] gives us, strung out with no interconnection, some of the main motifs of the following twenty-two pages."[5] Stuart Gilbert[6] and L. A. G. Strong[7] attempt to interpret this passage in a similar manner. Harry Levin's explanation of these two pages as a "thematic index to the following pages" is based on the same idea.[8] Like Curtius, Levin holds that the thematic prelude must remain meaningless without knowledge of what follows. If this were the whole truth, then the reader could safely skip over these two pages on first reading and perhaps return to them when he had read the entire chapter. In this case why did not Joyce put this word-motif collection at the end of the chapter?

In his search for new structural forms for the novel Joyce was stimulated in many ways by musical forms. Ezra Pound held that the overall structure of *Ulysses* takes the form of a sonata.[9] Stuart Gilbert, whose commentary owes much to the assistance of Joyce himself, calls the form of the whole "Sirens" chapter a "Fuga per canonem."[10]

Every literary work which is formed in analogy to musical forms raises the question of the relationship of the sound and meaning of words. To what extent is the sound element of language—the external body of the word and the sentence rhythm—capable of independent meaningful expression when detached from the words' meaning? To what extent can literature employ the analogy to music, for example, in the leitmotivic use of word-motifs which have been isolated from the context of language and content? Such considerations reveal basic differences between the expressive potential of literature and music which lend support to Curtius' critical reservations concerning the prelude to "Sirens." Curtius holds that this experiment is unsuccessful because Joyce overlooked the fact "that a musical motif is complete in itself and aesthetically satisfying; . . . The word-motif, on the other hand, is a meaningless fragment and only acquires its meaning in a concrete context."[11] Like the other commentators of this passage, however, Curtius overlooks the fact that Joyce did not stop at a simple musical analogy. Joyce did take into account the "deep essential difference between sounds and words"[12] by placing the prelusive word-motifs of this overture in a completely new, independent structure of meaning. At this point the evidence of such a structure can only be provided for a part of the prelude; this will suffice, however, to support the assumption of analogous relationships in the remaining part:

> And a call, pure, long and throbbing. Longindying call.
> Decoy. Soft word. But look! The bright stars fade. O rose! Notes chirruping answer. Castille. The morn is breaking. .
> Jingle jingle jaunted jingling.
> Coin rang. Clock clacked.

Avowal. *Sonnez.* I could. Rebound of garter. Not leave thee. Smack. *La cloche!* Thigh smack. Avowal. Warm. Sweetheart, goodbye. (p. 252)

The word-motifs of this section from the prelude to "Sirens" manifest the succession of motifs and the external structure of meaning of an alba or morning song. A large part of the rather fixed set of motifs of this type of lyric reappears here[13]:

1. The call or song of the watchman on the tower: "And a call, pure, long and throbbing. Longindying call."

2. The announcement of daybreak: "The bright stars fade." "The morn is breaking."

3. Portrayal of the protestations of love and the last caress: "Avowal. *Sonnez.* I could. Rebound of garter. Not leave thee. Smack. *La cloche!* Thigh smack. Avowal. Warm."

4. Departure of the knight: "Sweetheart, goodbye!"

There remain several word-motifs which need not necessarily be considered a part of this structure of meaning, but which can be included here without difficulty: "Decoy. Soft word" alludes to the secrecy of the love affair in the morning song. "Notes chirruping answer" can be understood as an allusion to the early song of the birds—a common motivic ornament in the morning song. "Jingle jingle jaunted jingling" is an onomatopoeic anticipation of the events of the next line; at the same time it is the word-leitmotif of the town cavalier Blazes Boylan, who is on his way in a coach to an intimate rendezvous with Mrs. Bloom while Bloom lingers in the Ormond. The insertion of this word-motif is one of Joyce's characteristic techniques. It serves as an indication of the ironic parallel between the events which are described in the medieval morning song and those in *Ulysses.*

This pasticcio of a morning song is, of course, one of the numerous stylistic and formal parodies in *Ulysses.* Although the parodistic intent is evident from the apparent formation of the poem from completely disparate elements, the real parody only becomes clear when the reader reencounters the same word-motifs in their original context in the chapter "Sirens." The content and values of the two structures of meaning come into contrast; there is a discrepancy between the ostensible meaning of the pasticcio and the meaning of the events presented in the bar of the Ormond. This discrepancy has an effect on the reader similar to the effect of the Homeric analogy which is employed throughout *Ulysses*. The contrast and the constant mirroring of two fundamentally different value systems supports the claim of the Bloom plot to universality; at the same time, however, the nobly heroic or lyrical world causes the everyday world to emerge fully in all its grotesque banality.[14] Several of the word-motifs from which the alba pasticcio is constructed actually undergo a grotesque process of redefinition when they are presented in the context of the chapter's events. The call of the watchman from the tower appears as the slowly dying tone of a tuning fork: "From the saloon a call came, long in dying. That was a tuning fork. . . . It throbbed, pure, purer, softly and softlier, its buzzing prongs. Longer in dying call" (p. 260). The protestations of love and the last caresses belong to the presentation of the erotic game with which a barmaid entertains her guests (p. 262).

The tendency to humoristic effect, occasionally even to distortion into the grotesque, is unmistakable; it is tied to the game of verbal expression in *Ulysses*. The experimental use of new structural forms also results frequently in a comical effect. Consider the next to the last chapter, which is based on the form of the catechism. A segment of life is presented with extreme realism of detail but with continuous comic treatment. This is doubtless in large measure an expression of Joyce's individual view of life. In one respect, however, a law of literary history of older periods appears to attain new validity here. The realistic presentation of the banal, everyday life of the lower classes was long considered by authors to be incapable of any but comic presentation. In Fielding's novels, for example, the narrative constantly falls into the comic or grotesque, often at the very moment when the action seems to take on serious or tragic aspects.[15] In a work where this realism of detail reaches an extreme form in the presentation of the everyday, of the banal, it may not be a complete coincidence that a comical undertone is audible. One could thus view *Ulysses* as further evidence that the "classical aesthetic rule of style which excluded any material realism from tragic or heroic works"[16] can still prove valid today.

The next chapter ("Cyclops—The Tavern") introduces another new narrative situation. The events in the tavern are presented as the first-person narrative of a regular customer who belongs to the typical circle of those who every afternoon begin to beseige the bars of Dublin. A narrator figure belonging to such a sharply defined type makes any further commentary or illumination of the scene superfluous. In literary history a parallel to this first-person narrative in the middle of a third-person narrative can be found in the interpolated story so popular in older novels. There, however, the first-person narrator always appears under the auspices of the author or authorial narrator, who makes appropriate preparations for the change of narrative situation. In *Ulysses* the transition from the third-person to the first-person form is not designated at all. In the first-person narrative, which portrays Bloom's argument with the "Citizen" in Barney Kiernan's pub, segments of stylistic parody occur which cannot be attributed to the first-person narrator. These stylistic parodies represent a grotesque, gigantically distorted continuation of the action of the first-person narrative ("The figure seated on a large boulder at the foot of a round tower was that of a broadshouldered deepchested stronglimbed . . . hero" [p. 291]). Such disillusive parody also contrasts sharply with the currently pressing questions of the Celtic Renaissance, with the image of Ireland in the feuilletons, and with spiritistic and folkloric cults. Here, too, a self-interpreting contrast relationship is created by means of the chapter's segmentation. More precisely, the realistic self-portrait of the Irish pub mentality contrasts with Ireland's ideal image, which already appears here in parodistic distortion and which in Joyce's time doubtless haunted many a hothead of the Irish Renaissance movement.

The next chapter ("Nausicaa—The Rocks") seems to begin as an authorial narrative. The authorial medium here, however, obviously wears a mask; it is imitating the narrative stance, feelings, and thoughts of a sentimental novelist. This chapter's scenes and figures appear to be taken directly from one of the literary mass productions which spring so abundantly from the fantasy of such authors. Later the presentation also penetrates into the consciousness of Gerty MacDowell and Bloom. This glimpse, as it were, behind the scenes of the sentimental idyll of an "evening on the strand" brings about a surprising reinterpretation of the scene. Thoughts, emotions, and desires which the author—writing with the mask of the sentimental novelist— could never have expected of his figures now well up in Gerty and Bloom. With the change of narrative situation from apparent authorial to figural presentation the unvarnished reality of the *Ulysses* world obtrudes before the sterotypical image of life in the subliterary mass novel. Here the technique of segmentation, joined with stylistic parody, develops into a new and effective structural form of the novel.

It is more difficult to view the similar technique of the next chapter ("Oxen of the Sun—The Hospital") as an enrichment of the novel's structural forms. Although one cannot fail to recognize the virtuosity of the pasticcio itself, one may still ask whether the author's expressive intention has achieved adequate formal realization. Evidently Joyce, who until now has avoided this trap again and again with great skill, falls prey after all to the "fallacy of imitative form." Stuart Gilbert gives the following guide for this chapter: "The rationale of this sequence of imitations lies in the theme. The *technic* and the subject of this episode are both *embryonic development* and the styles of prose employed follow an exact historical order."[17] The chapter is made up of a series of segments. The abrupt beginning which usually distinguishes the segment technique is lacking here, but the individual segments are clearly set off from one another by the various imitative styles. In each segment the authorial medium conceals itself behind the mask of a different literary personality—Bunyan, Sterne, Carlyle, Meredith, and so forth. In this way a series of pasticci portrays the development of English prose style. The intended parallel between the development of the human embryo—the scene of the action is Dublin's maternity hospital—and the development of English prose, however, is rendered too literally.

The chapter "Circe—The Brothel" takes the form of a dramatic procession. The extensive descriptions which accompany the dramatic dialogue in the manner of stage directions represent a substratum of epic presentation. In these passages the individual figures of the procession are described in detail. In part they also report the progress of the dramatic action; the unity of the chapter's meaning only arises from the conjunction of the two parts, the dramatic-scenic and the epic part. The form of the dramatic procession was chosen in order to differentiate the dream-hallucination of this Walpurgis-Night chapter from the epically formed, reality-oriented parts of the rest of the novel. The content of Bloom's and Stephen's hallucinations and nightmares is objectified through the dramatic form. In this way the border between the real and imagined experiences of these two figures in the Nighttown district of Dublin also remains undetermined. Thus, for example, Bloom's arrival at Bella Cohen's house (p. 466), the first appearance of the real Bella Cohen (p. 515), or the episode in which Stephen smashes the chandelier in her house (pp. 567–68) are presented and described in the same manner as the real events which accompany these dream events.

The chapter "Eumaeus—The Shelter" shows most clearly the inadequacy of many of the categories applied by Stuart Gilbert to the individual chapters. According to Gilbert the predominant technique of this chapter is "narrative (old)," which supposedly mirrors, as the first chapter of the third part, the "narrative (young)" technique of the first chapter of the first part. Yet there is hardly any similarity between the narrative situations of these two chapters. The narrative situation in "Eumaeus" could be compared more readily with the beginning of the Gerty Mac-Dowell episode. In both places an authorial medium narrates; both times it wears a mask which alters its real features. In this chapter it assumes the features of a reporter who is writing for a stylistically ambitious provincial newspaper.[18] In interpreting this chapter it is important to recognize this guise of the authorial medium, for only this guise reveals the irony of carelessly dwelling upon inconsequental trivialities and of the often very circumstantial formulations. The presentation of Bloom's and Stephen's actions, too, can only be understood in the light of the unreal face of the narrator. In addition the chapter parodistically imitates the stereotypical narrative embellishments of pedantic reportlike style; the chapter repeatedly inserts empty phrases such as "aforesaid," "and so forth and so on," and "to cut a long story short" into the narration.[19] The authorial narrative situation is also imitated by the rendition of Bloom's consciousness not in the form of an interior monologue, that is, in the first person, but rather in the third person.

The end of the chapter brings yet another strange confusion of the narrative situation. The commentaries have maintained unanimous silence concerning it. As the two figures Bloom and Stephen, very much in need of rest and sleep, stagger homeward, they encounter a sweeper car. From this point on the narrative becomes more and more sluggish and a good deal of chaff is milled, as if the authorial narrator, too, were now only speaking automatically, in a drowsed condition:

> The driver never said a word, good, bad or indifferent. He merely watched the two figures, as he sat on his lowbacked car, both black—one full, one lean—walk towards the railway bridge, *to be married by Father Maher.* As they walked, they at times stopped and walked again, continuing their *tête-à-tête* (which of course he was utterly out of), about sirens, enemies of man's reason, mingled with a number of other topics of the same category, usurpers, historical cases of the kind while the man in the sweeper car or you might as well call it in the sleeper car who in any case couldn't possibly hear because they were too far simply sat in his seat near the end of lower Gardiner street *and looked after their lowbacked car.* (p. 649)

This confused paragraph is partially explained if one assumes that the narrator is acting as if he were falling asleep. At first he tries to get himself past a yawning chasm in his thoughts by speaking with empty phrases; then he allows more and more automatic associations to flow into his speech. Initially these phrases have a certain comic effect ("sleeper car"), but finally they no longer make any sense at all ("their lowbacked car"). It seems reasonable to see behind this portrait of My Uncle Toby as narrator a parody of the conventional authorial novel's narrative mode and its frequently flagrant disregard of formal discipline. The drowsy narrator in this passage must continually correct himself in his choice of viewpoint ("which of course he was utterly out of"); he gives rein in the narrative to his half-dreaming consciousness. Many authors behave in the very same way—in Joyce's view—when they produce, enraptured by the sound of their own voices, thick-tome opuses. Coming from an author who could set the laconic line "Triest-Zürich-Paris 1914–1921" at the end of his novel, this criticism is doubtless to be taken seriously.

There is little to be said about the penultimate chapter. It is the *point de mire*[20] of all hostile critics. The external form of an examination paper,[21] according to which the content of the chapter is recapitulated in questions and answers, can hardly be regarded as an enrichment of the expressive possibilities of the novel. Nevertheless, the chapter is very effective as a formal or stylistic parody. The authorial medium, which here provides both questions and answers, wears the masks of the pedantic schoolmaster and his overzealous pupil.

The last chapter, the long monologue of Molly Bloom's consciousness, can be viewed as a consistent example of a first-person narrative in which the narrative process is not designated in any way. Here this form will be called interior monologue. No narrator meditating between the stream of Molly Bloom's consciousness and the reader, no narrating self can be perceived. The absence of any punctuation and the flowing together of syntactic units strengthen the impression that the reader is receiving a direct glimpse into Molly Bloom's consciousness. There is no longer any question of "narrating."

The frequent critical objection that language is not capable of rendering the processes of human consciousness will be discussed in more detail in the next chapter. It is a fact that the literary work of art can reproduce only human speech with any degree of precision. All other processes can only be presented in a stylized condition. Any new style of presentation is literally justified, however, if it is able to awaken in the reader the impression that by this process of presentation reality is captured with only slight distortion of the image. The author who experiments is doubtless aware that he, too, can only provide a symbol, but no immediate copy of reality. With the help of a new method, misleadingly labelled "realistic," an effect can often be achieved which would not have been possible for traditional methods of presentation. This new method of presentation can then safely prove itself basically unrealistic; this does not diminish its expressive potential. Compare, for example, the self-presentation of Moll Flanders with Molly Bloom's monologue. Both methods of presentation were considered "realistic"; both, however, are stylizations of reality—with very different methods, of course. More than two centuries of continuously developing narrative technique lie between these two self-presentations, yet it would be difficult to decide which self-portrait should be considered "more realistic."

Examination of the individual chapters has shown that the narrative situation in *Ulysses* is established anew in almost every chapter. Since the narrative begins anew at the start of each chapter, the reader is prepared to a certain extent for a change in the narrative orientation. For this reason the change of narrative situation from chapter to chapter will not impair the reader's illusion. On the other hand, it is quite unusual in narrative literature to change the narrative situation within the context of narration; this can be observed continually in *Ulysses*. In the following quotation from the chapter "Wandering Rocks —The Streets" the inserted numbers indicate a third-person narrative situation [3] or a first-person narrative situation [1]:

[3] From the sundial towards James's Gate walked Mr Kernan pleased with the order he had booked for Pulbrook Robertson boldly along James's street, past Shackleton's offices.

[1] Got round him all right. How do you do, Mr Crimmins? First rate, sir. I was afraid you might be up in your other establishment in Pimlico. How are things going? Just keeping alive. Lovely weather we are having. Yes, indeed. Good for the country. Those farmers are always grumbling. I'll just take a thimbleful of your best gin, Mr Crimmins. A small gin, sir. Yes, sir. Terrible affair that General Slocum explosion. Terrible, terrible! A thousand casualties. And heartrending scenes. Men trampling down women and children. Most brutal thing. What do they say was the cause? Spontaneous combustion: most scandalous revelation. Not a single lifeboat would float and the firehose all burst. What I can't understand is how the inspectors ever allowed a boat like that . . . Now you are talking straight, Mr Crimmins. You know why? Palmoil. Is that a fact? Without a doubt. Well now, look at that. And America they say is the land of the free. I thought we were bad here.

[1] I smiled at him. *America*, I said, quietly, just like that. *What is it? The sweepings of every country including our own. Isn't that true?* That's a fact.

Graft, my dear sir. Well, of course, where there's money going there's always someone to pick it up.

Saw him looking at my frockcoat. Dress does it. Nothing like a dressy appearance. Bowls them over.

[3] —Hello, Simon, Father Cowley said. How are things?

—Hello, Bob, old man, Mr. Dedalus answered stopping.

[3] Mr Kernan halted and preened himself before the sloping mirror of Peter Kennedy, hairdresser. [1] Stylish coat, beyond a doubt. Scott of Dawson street. Well worth the half sovereign I gave Neary for it. Never built under three guineas. Fits me down to the ground. Some Kildare street club toff had it probably. John Mulligan, the manager of the Hibernian bank, gave me a very sharp eye yesterday on Carlisle bridge as if he remembered me.

[1] Aham! Must dress the character for those fellows. Knight of the road. Gentleman. And now, Mr Crimmins, may we have the honour of your custom again, sir. The cup that cheers but not inebriates, as the old saying has it.

[3] North wall and sir John Rogerson's quay, with hulls and anchorchains, sailing westward, sailed by a skiff, a crumpled throwaway, rocked on the ferry-wash, Elijah is coming.

[3] Mr Kernan glanced in farewell at his image. [1 or 3] High colour, of course. Grizzled moustache. Returned Indian officer.

[3] Bravely he bore his stumpy body forward on spatted feet,

squaring his shoulders. [3] Is that Lambert's brother over the way, Sam? What? Yes. He's as like it as damn it. No. The windscreen of that motorcar in the sun there. Just a flash like that. Damn like him. (pp. 235–37)

No attention is paid to the narrative convention which demands that in a unified narrative reference is made to figures either in the third person throughout or in the first person throughout. Direct address and interpolated stories in which the author lets a figure speak are naturally exceptions. This passage begins with a third-person reference to Mr. Kernan, the scene's main figure. But with the sentence: "Got round to him all right," a first-person reference emerges. There is no clear indication of the first person, such as a personal pronoun. As narrated monologue, this sentence could be a third-person reference. Narrated monologue, however, would here require the verb to be in the past-perfect tense. There follows a passage of dialogue which is conceivable in a third-person narrative as well as in a first-person narrative. The beginning of the next paragraph ("I smiled at him") returns to a clear first-person narrative situation. This situation is immediately followed by an interpolated segment which focuses on a simultaneous meeting between Simon Dedalus and Father Cowley. The presentation then returns in the third-person form to Mr. Kernan, only to change after one sentence back into the first-person form of an interior monologue. Then follows a short passage of dialogue in which the words of the two speakers are even joined at one point in a single sentence: "And now, Mr Crimmins" (the speaker is Mr. Kernan), "may we have the honour of your custom again, sir" (the speaker is Mr. Crimmins). Once again the perspective rises to an authorial panorama: a discarded leaflet which announces the arrival of an evangelist preacher is floating on the Liffey toward the harbor and the open sea. Mr. Kernan is unaware of these events. In the next sentence it is reported that he is still standing before the mirror at the barber's. This account in the third person is followed by a presentation of the thoughts which come to Mr. Kernan while he stands regarding his reflection in the mirror. Since in the staccato style characteristic of the rendering of consciousness verbs and pronouns are absent, it is not possible to determine whether this represents part of a narrated monologue or part of an interior monologue. After a short report of one sentence ("Bravely he bore . . .") another segment is inserted which consists of a fragment of a conversation held between two unspecified figures. It contains a reference to one more of the work's numerous meetings, by means of which Joyce wants to express the simultaneity of a number of events in various parts of the city.

Unity of narrative situation presupposes a fixed central point which is presented as a constant and which radiates orientation; this point can lie either in a narrator who shows himself personally; in the consciousness of a figure; or in an imaginary observer of the scene. In *Ulysses* this central point or this center of gravity no longer exists. The resulting narrative conventions— unity of the first-person or third-person reference, fixed perspective and point of observation, etc.—have thus become irrelevant. The reader who has once been weaned of the help of these narrative conventions will no longer find the reading of *Ulysses* difficult in this respect. The real difficulty of *Ulysses* lies in quite another area, namely in the unattainable feat of memory which is constantly required of the reader; word-motifs, conversation fragments, segmentlike scenes must be identified and understood according to their proper place.[22]

In *Ulysses* Joyce did not intend to compete with the formative possibilities of the conventional novel. Such an intention could never justify the loss of clarity, structural transparency, and general readability about which so many readers of *Ulysses* complain. Joyce's intention was directed at a task which the novel in its traditional forms simply could not accomplish. The events on a certain day in Dublin, the conversations, thoughts, experiences of several characters—all this represents only the foreground. Behind this one sees the mental process by which a partly serious, partly playful consciousness occupies itself with the imaginative complex "June 16, 1904, in Dublin." If one views *Ulysses* as a monologue in which the author conceives the work, one can see the meaningful unity of both the overall structure and the specific techniques of presentation. Such a conceptual monologue relates to the presentation of a story by an authorial narrator in the same way that the presentation of a stream of consciousness, where an experience seems to become visible *in actu,* relates to the report of an authorial narrator recreating events in retrospect.

The idea that *Ulysses* can be understood as a monologue can already be found in C. G. Jung's discussion of the work. Strangely enough, this explanation has found little echo among critics of *Ulysses.* In his article "Ulysses. Ein Monolog"[23] Jung interprets the entire novel as the stream of consciousness of one figure, whom he calls Ulysses, and behind whom it is not difficult to recognize the creative consciousness of the author. "I must confess I suspect that this Ulysses figure, acting as a more comprehensive self, is the corresponding subject to all the objects under the glass slide; he is the being which acts as if it were Mr. Bloom or a printing shop or a crumpled piece of paper, while in reality it is 'the dark hidden father' of its objects."[24] This subject is never concentrated into a tangible, corporeal phenomenon, but its voice can be heard here and there. Associations which have formed in its consciousness rise to the surface; his memory touches the notes of past material. The subject for the world of *Ulysses* is simply the author's consciousness at the moment of the process of conception. It is characteristic of this type of subject that it suppresses any explicit reference to itself, whereas in the presentation of an authorial narrator abundant use is made of such references. Unlike the monologue in the drama or the interior monologue, the conceptual monologue is not primarily a means of self-expression, but rather a stage in the work's development; it expresses the process of the author's objective formation of a world. It is therefore not the personal self of the monologizing author, but a dramatized self, the creative consciousness of the artist.

If one keeps in mind this explanation of the plan and structure of *Ulysses*, then many peculiarities of the presentation become more comprehensible. The course of the main strand of action, for example, is constantly interrupted by the lightening-like flashes of scenic fragments; these serve to indicate simultaneous, distant events which are tied to the main action only by association. The author's imagination, which aims for the coexistence of all events, does not adhere to the unity and continuity of a single strand of action. Even during the course of individual scenes phases of the action appear which are not refracted through the consciousness of any of the figures present, although these phases resemble the contents of consciousness—above all the characteristic associative connection of the parts. This is especially clear in the "Sirens" chapter. The organization of the word-motifs in the prelude to this chapter reveals a stream of consciousness. The segmentation of numerous chapters corresponds to the abrupt alternation with which the consciousness takes up relationships and drops them again. Since the narrative form is still in progress, unity of narrative situation, which is the external sign of completed internal organization, is not yet attained. First-person and third-person references still alternate, depending on whether the author distances himself from or temporarily identifies with a figure. For this author the individual consciousness of a figure does not represent an inviolable unit. For this reason there is an active exchange of motifs, thoughts, images, associations between the figures, even though this shared part of the contents of consciousness is nowhere communicated externally. Bloom and Stephen even share a significant portion of the Walpurgis-Night phantasmagoria. In the chapter "Circe—The Brothel" there is no longer any demarcation of the border between hallucination and experienced reality. Finally, the frequent transformation of the figure in which the narrator appears (in the chapters with apparent authorial narration) could also be explained with the help of the conceptual monologue hypothesis. The creative consciousness seems to disguise itself as various narrator types in order to ascertain the way such a typical sensibility can affect the material, like a given lighting effect on a scene.

Ulysses is the presentation of the author's creative condition resulting from the idea "June 16, 1904, in Dublin." The presentational conventions of this novel are the laws of creative mental effort. Unlike any author before him Joyce revealed with *Ulysses* the immense demands made on the intellect and imagination of an author in the act of conception and composition. At the same time Joyce attained with this novel the very last stage in the continuous formal scale of the epical mode. Perhaps he has even gone beyond this stage, which he defined as follows in the words of Stephen in *A Portrait of the Artist as a Young Man* (1916), that is, at a time when little more existed of *Ulysses* than a vague plan and a few fragments:

> The simplest epical form is seen emerging out of lyrical literature when the artist prolongs and broods upon himself as the centre of an epical event and this form progresses till the centre of emotional gravity is equidistant from the artist himself and from others. The narrative is no longer purely personal. The personality of the artist passes into the narration itself, flowing round and round the persons and the action like a vital sea.   (p. 244)

VI

EXCURSUS: THE RENDERING

OF CONSCIOUSNESS

IN ANTICIPATION IT SHOULD BE STATED from the very first that "realistic" presentation of a figure's consciousness is impossible in literature. The portion of the contents of consciousness which does emerge in the presentation is stylized; it suggests or symbolizes the events of consciousness, but does not reproduce them. The accomplishment of those authors who are considered pioneers of the rendering of consciousness in the modern novel—their forerunners are not only Henry James and Gustav Flaubert, but authors of all periods—cannot justly be evaluated according to the degree of "realistic" reproduction they have attained. Each individual work must be judged according to the literary effectiveness of its stylization of consciousness in the corresponding period of literary history. To the extent that the attempts of Dorothy Richardson, Edouard Dujardin, James Joyce, Virginia Woolf, and many others are subordinated to the narrative situation and to the predominant stylistic level of the individual novel, these attempts satisfy the reader's illusion expectancy and are thus literarily justified.

A novel in which the character's dialogue is rendered realistically—speech being the only process which can be "reproduced" literarily with any accuracy—must turn to more complex means of stylizing consciousness than a novel which has its characters speak only in syntactically polished sentences. In a novel of the latter kind the contents of consciousness can be sufficiently characterized by the same features which appear in the dialogue of the first type: short, incomplete sentences; truncation of forms and syntax; neologisms; and so on.

The choice of the mode of stylization which should be used to render consciousness also depends on the narrative situation. An authorial narrator will generally refrain from an intimate presentation of his characters' consciousness. In the figural novel, on the other hand, a figure's consciousness can be presented in detail and in a particular style, such as a staccato style or one which suggests the stream of consciousness. Wyndham Lewis attempts to reject the staccato style used by Joyce to characterize the contents of consciousness. Lewis compares Joyce's technique with Dickens' realistic reproduction of Mr. Jingle's speech in the *Pickwick Papers*, but the similarity he sees between the two is misleading.[1] In the works compared there are completely different presentational conventions at work which give the individual stylistic techniques completely different meanings. Since, moreover, a realistic reproduction of the contents of consciousness can never be the intention of a literary presentation, the similarity of Mr. Jingle's speech with Mr. Bloom's consciousness basically does not prove anything. The literary significance of a given form of rendering consciousness can only be evaluated in the light of the work's predominant narrative situation.

The authorial novel reveals the characters' consciousness only in the form of complete thoughts and in full sentences. Aside from the expression of such thoughts in report form there is no specific characterization of the contents of consciousness:

> In fact, when Partridge *came to ruminate* on the relation he had heard from Jones, he could not reconcile to himself that Mr. Allworthy should turn his son (for so he most firmly *believed* him to be) out of doors, for any reason which he had heard assigned. He *concluded* therefore, that the whole was a fiction, and that Jones, of whom he had often from his correspondents heard the wildest character, had in reality run away from his father. It *came into his head*, therefore, that . . . (*Tom Jones*, Book VIII, Chapter VII [italics are mine]).

This kind of thought report seems to be formed in analogy to indirect discourse. In both cases the narrator's voice, which can be perceived at all times, is superimposed upon the individual, personal aspects of the character. It therefore becomes necessary continually to provide signals which identify what is reported as speech or as the contents of consciousness or as the thoughts of a figure. In indirect discourse this takes place by the insertion of *verba dicendi* and by the use of the subjunctive or a shift in tense. In the thought report this is accomplished by the continual insertion of formulae such as those indicated by italics in the above passage. In the cases of indirect discourse and the thought report the spoken or thought material is presented from a standpoint of posteriority. The report form used in this situation for the rendering of consciousness is also employed, however, for the narration of external events.

Once the findings of psychology had called attention to the special laws governing the processes of consciousness, this form no longer seemed adequate, especially if the author was attempting to express the peculiar inner organization of consciousness. Earlier authors, of course, already attempted to distinguish the thought report as such by the use of appropriate stylization. As a result the staccato style of rendering consciousness can already be found occasionally in authors of the eighteenth and nineteenth centuries. More important, however, are two forms of rendering consciousness which developed from the narrative situations of the first-person and the figural novel—interior monologue and narrated monologue.

Interior monologue, also called *stiller Monolog* or *monologue intérieur*, corresponds to the narrative situation of the first-person novel. If the narrating self in a first-person novel withdraws so far that the experiencing self with its feelings and thoughts seems to appear with no narrative mediation before the reader's eyes, then the first-person novel, too, becomes capable of directly rendering consciousness; it becomes an interior monologue. The interior monologue displays a figure's stream of consciousness as if this stream were not being guided or directed by any narrative act. In this way the presentation attains the immediacy which the reader's illusion expectancy requires for the rendering of consciousness. The advantages of interior monologue, which also has many traits in common with direct discourse, are quite apparent. Interior monologue permits extensive characterization of the idiosyncrasy of consciousness, just as direct address makes it possible to express the dialect coloration, the characteristic choice of words, and individual sentence structure in the speech of a figure.

In his novel *The Sound and the Fury* William Faulkner employs a kind of interior monologue for the rendering of consciousness. The novel consists of four parts in which the life of the Compson family is presented. The first two parts are exclusively the interior monologue of two of the Compson children, the feeble-minded Benjy and the suicidal Quentin. This interior monologue also incorporates all dialogue which occurs. The time of action of each monologue is restricted to a few hours of a given day. The contents of each of the two figures' consciousness are permeated by numerous memories, associations, and so forth, however, so that indirectly a much larger span of time is encompassed—not only the history of the Compsons on these two days, but during several decades. With the help of the interior monologue Faulkner succeeds in revealing the individual differences between the processes of consciousness of such opposing character types as the feeble-minded person and the Harvard freshman. Faulkner puts the verb of the interior monologue in the epic preterite. This tense lends the interior monologue something of the aspect of a retrospection on the part of the monologizing character. In order to avoid the appearance of this sort of guidance and control of the interior monologue many authors prefer to use the present tense rather than the epic preterite. The present tense is used, for example, in Arthur Schnitzler's *Leutnant Gustl*, in Dujardin's *Les Lauriers sont coupés* and in Molly Bloom's closing monologue in Joyce's *Ulysses*.

Dujardin called the technique used by him for rendering consciousness in *Les Lauriers sont coupés* "monologue intérieur."[2]

This concept appeared before Dujardin's essay, however, in an essay on James Joyce written by Valéry Larbaud.[3] In English literary criticism "interior monologue" is almost always equated with William James's concept of the "stream of consciousness."[4] Lawrence E. Bowling has attempted to distinguish between the two in respect to the depth reached by the presentation of consciousness. For him stream of consciousness means "that narrative method by which the author attempts to give *a direct quotation of the mind*—not merely of the language area but of the whole consciousness." For the rendering of the contents of consciousness in the "language area" he chooses the concept of "interior monologue." To these two he adds "internal analysis," by which he means the authorial presentation of the thoughts of a figure, the thought report.[5] The distinction between the first two concepts is valueless in practice, as any attempt to apply them will show. Is Molly Bloom's monologue still interior monologue or already stream of consciousness? The contents of Molly Bloom's consciousness are presented with the help of conventional vocabulary and normal word forms, but the larger syntactic units are fused into a single monstrous sentence. Does this overstep the boundary of the "language area" or not? Bowling also disregards the fact that the concept of interior monologue refers to a literary form. Stream of consciousness, on the other hand, is primarily used to attribute a specific quality to the processes of consciousness. William James originally coined the term in this sense:

> Consciousness, then, does not appear to itself chopped up in bits. Such words as "chain" or "train" do not describe it fitly as it presents itself in the first instance. It is nothing jointed; it flows. A "river" or "stream" are the metaphors by which it is most naturally described. *In talking of it hereafter, let us call it the stream of thought, of consciousness, or of subjective life.*
>
> (*The Principles of Psychology*, vol. I, p. 239)

The concept of stream of consciousness should therefore be used to characterize this peculiarity of consciousness. An interior monologue can also have the features of a stream of consciousness, as does Molly Bloom's interior monologue in *Ulysses*. A stream of consciousness can likewise appear in the third-person form. Numerous examples of this can be found in the novels of Virginia Woolf.

In the figural novel the reader views the fictional world in the mirror of the figural medium's consciousness. The rendering of consciousness thus becomes the main concern of this novel form. For the figural narrative situation the corresponding form for rendering consciousness is the narrated monologue.* Both are characterized by the withdrawal of the narrator and by the reader's illusion that he is receiving a direct glimpse into the consciousness of a figure. The general analogy between the presentation of speech and the presentation of consciousness has already been drawn specifically for the relationship between direct discourse and interior monologue and between indirect discourse and the thought report. This can now be extended to a third form of speech presentation, narrated discourse, which corresponds to narrated monologue as a form for the rendering of consciousness.

The term narrated monologue will be used here to refer to the narrated monologue as a form for the presentation of consciousness. The concept of narrated monologue also includes what Bernhard Fehr called "substitutionary narration" and "substitutionary perception." Fehr illustrates the concept with the help of the following examples:

1. On turning round Fred saw Jack coming across the street towards him.
2. "Look!" Fred turned round. Jack was coming across the street towards him.[6]

---

* Stanzel takes pains to differentiate between two kinds of *erlebte Rede*— one used to render speech and one used to render thought. This difficulty was eliminated in the translation by using two different terms, "narrated discourse" and "narrated monologue." Here I have followed the suggested terminology of Dorrit Cohn, "Narrated Monologue: Definition of a Fictional Style," *Comparative Literature*, XVIII (1966), 97–112. It may be added that the French term is *style indirect libre*; the Russian is *nesobstvenno-prjamaja reč'*. The use of this English terminology has brought about several slight changes in the text.—Translator's note.

Fehr calls no. 1 a report; this corresponds to the concept of the "thought report" which has been used here. No. 2 is an example of substitutionary perception, which here will be taken as a subcategory of the main concept of narrated monologue. It is understandable from the narrative situation of the figural novel that constant use must be made of this kind of narrated monologue, since it is almost always the perceptions and thoughts of a figure which are portrayed rather than a narrator's report of these perceptions and thoughts. In the following passage from *The Ambassadors* Strether, the novel's figural medium, occupies his thoughts with the impression made on him by Jeanne de Vionnet. This is followed by a series of thoughts of which only the first is introduced by the word thought"; the rest appear as narrated monologue:

> She was fairly beautiful to him—a faint pastel in an oval frame: he thought of her already as of some lurking image in a long gallery, the portrait of a small old-time princess of whom nothing was known but that she had died young. Little Jeanne wasn't, doubtless, to die young, but one couldn't, all the same, bear on her lightly enough. It was bearing hard, it was bearing as *he*, in any case, wouldn't bear, to concern himself, in relation to her, with the question of a young man. Odious, really, the question of a young man; one didn't treat such a person as a maid-servant suspected of a "follower." And then young men, young men—well, the thing was their business simply, or was, at all events, hers. She was fluttered, fairly fevered—to the point of a little glitter that came and went in her eyes and a pair of pink spots that stayed in her cheeks—with the great adventure of dining out and with the greater one still, possibly, of finding a gentleman whom she must think of as very, very old, a gentleman with eyeglasses, wrinkles, a long, grizzled mustache.

> (pp. 180–81)

The predominating figural narrative situation causes the reader to imagine that he is experiencing a direct glimpse into Strether's consciousness. For this reason the entire paragraph and almost the entire novel appear as the substitutionary perception of Strether. An occasional intrusion by the narrator, such as the word "thought" in the second sentence, does not affect the narrative situation, which Percy Lubbock has described as "looking down upon a mind grown visible."[7] The author as narrator has become a mere "holder of a verbal mirror."[8] The reader concretizes only the image in the verbal mirror; the author as narrator no longer gains admittance to the reader's imagination. Werner Günther speaks of a synthetic act of "internal vision" and "external vision" on the part of the author and the reader; this act takes place in the narrated monologue.[9] A unification takes place between objectivity and subjectivity of expression, between distanced broad survey of the material and dramatic experience of it. This is made possible by the peculiar position which the narrated monologue holds between direct discourse and report or indirect discourse.[10] In narrated monologue, as in indirect discourse and in the report, the bearer of consciousness or speaker is named in the third person. Despite this third-person reference, however, in narrated monologue the individual traits in the speech or thought of a figure are not fully effaced, as is generally the case in the indirect presentation of speech. Consider, for example, the following sentence from the last quotation: "And then young men—well, the thing was their business simply, or was, at all events, hers." Although reference is made to Strether only in the third person throughout the novel, such a sentence gives the impression that he is formulating these thoughts in the first person. In the authorial novel this kind of direct self-expression of thoughts is restricted to the narrator who actually narrates in the first-person form and comments on the narrated material. In the figural novel the direct presentation of the contents of consciousness of a third-person figure— in the form of narrated monologue—is general practice.

The verb in narrated monologue as a form for the presentation of consciousness is usually in the preterite. Yet since in a long presentation of consciousness in narrated monologue the reader's center of orientation lies in the now-and-here of the bearer of consciousness, as can be seen in the above passage, the epic preterite has the imaginative value of the present. This explains the frequency with which temporal designations are made from the point of view of a figure and its respective experiential present, rather than from the point of view of the author. The same holds true for the designations of place in such a narrative situation. In the figural novel the "I" or *hic* deixis of the figural medium everywhere suppresses the third-person orientation which would otherwise be created by the narrator, from whose standpoint this figure is designated as "he." "Fiction is the one epistemological region where the first-person originity, the subjectivity of a third person (as a third person) can be presented."[11] Käte Hamburger's important observation is valid, strictly speaking, only for the figural novel, for only there is the "first-person originity" of a figure presented without disruption. In the authorial novel the spatio-temporal orientation can maintain itself only for short stretches in the now-and-here of a figure.

In the authorial novel everything enters the reader's imagination from the point of view of the narrator. Insofar as the narrated material is not scenically dramatized, it appears in the form of a report, polished, stripped of all excessive impulses, arranged with a narrative goal in view, always as something complete and finished. In the form of the first-person novel, too, one always hears the reflective retrospective tone which in itself causes the more important contours of the presentation to emerge more strongly. This tone gives the seemingly directionless movement of the action a definiteness which at least suggests the existence of some ultimate goal. Many materials and themes can only attain final, valid formation in one of these two types of novel. This is especially true for material which demands a narrator's ruling vision, his formative power to compress material into clear lines of development. Examples of this are to be seen in the novel of education, the *Bildungsroman*, and in the developmental novel. The figural novel with extensive presentation of consciousness, on the other hand, can offer adequate formal expression to material whose external action is, or can be, limited to a short span of time. In this form all events must also be capable of being mirrored sufficiently from the observation point of a "central intelligence." This observation point, the figural medium of the novel, allows the reader to look into its consciousness; this means that the contents of this consciousness seem to be revealed to the reader without authorial mediation or without the self-censorship of the "I" which manifests itself consciously (i.e. the narrating self in the first-person novel). The dramatization of consciousness is the most prominent formative possibility offered by this narrative situation with its corresponding use of narrated monologue to render consciousness. A figure's thoughts, decisions, and feelings can be shown in their interplay, in their fluctuations, and in their conflict with one another.

Three possibilities for rendering consciousness in the novel have been distinguished here: thought report or internal analysis, interior monologue, and the presentation of consciousness in narrated monologue. These three forms for the rendering of consciousness are analogous to the three forms of speech presentation: indirect discourse, direct discourse, and narrated discourse. They correspond closely, moreover, to the three narrative situations of the novel: the authorial, the first-person, and the figural narrative situations. This does not imply that each individual form for the rendering of consciousness is possible in only one narrative situation. As a rule interior monologue, to be sure, can only be readily incorporated into the first-person novel. Narrated monologue, however, is also employed occasionally in the authorial novel, as Lisa Glauser has demonstrated for the predominantly authorial novels of the Victorian period.[12] On the other hand the thought report is not restricted to the authorial novel; in the figural novel it can alternate with narrated monologue. In general, however, the thought report will predominate in the authorial novel and narrated monologue in the figural novel.

It has been shown that in Joyce's *Ulysses* there is no unified narrative situation. As a result the forms for rendering consciousness are also in constant flux. The last chapter of the novel consists solely of an interior monologue. In the authorial chapters, for example in the first half of "Nausicaa—The Rocks" and in all of "Eumaeus—The Shelter," the thought report predominates. In the nighttown episode of "Circe" the processes of Stephen's and Bloom's consciousness are personified and dramatized; this form of rendering consciousness is not basically characteristic of the novel.

Most instructive, however, are the first chapters of the novel, for here Joyce opens new paths in the presentation of consciousness. It has been shown that the first six chapters consist of predominantly figural presentation. According to the narrative situation one would expect narrated monologue and occasionally the thought report to be the forms used for rendering consciousness. These two forms are employed frequently, but the predominant presentation of consciousness appears in interior monologue. This is shown clearly in the following passage from the third chapter of *Ulysses*. Stephen has finished giving his history lesson and now strolls on the Dublin strand. During the presentation of his walk objective observation constantly shifts into subjective perception. When Stephen's subjective perceptions have as their content things or processes which can also be regarded as objectively perceived, these perceptions appear in the form of narrated monologue. Thoughts which are evoked in his consciousness as a result of these perceptions or by free association are rendered in the form of interior monologue:

The grainy sand had gone from under his feet. His boots trod again a damp crackling mast, razorshells, squeaking pebbles, that on the unnumbered pebbles beats, wood sieved by the shipworm, lost Armada. Unwholesome sandflats waited to suck his treading soles, breathing upward sewage breath. He coasted them, walking warily. A porter-bottle stood up, stogged to its waist, in the cakey sand dough. A sentinel: isle of dreadful thirst. Broken hoops on the shore; at the land a maze of dark cunning nets; farther away chalkscrawled backdoors and on the higher beach a dryingline with two crucified shirts. Ringsend: wigwams of brown steersmen and master mariners. Human shells.

He halted. I have passed the way to aunt Sara's. Am I not going there? Seems not. No-one about. He turned northeast and crossed the firmer sand towards the Pigeonhouse.

—*Qui vous a mis dans cette fichue position?*

—*C'est le pigeon, Joseph.*

> Patrice, home on furlough, lapped warm milk with me in the bar MacMahon. Son of the wild goose, Kevin Egan of Paris. My father's a bird, he lapped the sweet *lait chaud* with pink young tongue, plump bunny's face. Lap, *lapin*. He hopes to win in the *gros lots*. About the nature of women he read in Michelet. But he must send me *La Vie de Jésus* by M. Leo Taxil. Lent it to his friend.   (pp. 41–42)

The figural medium of this passage, Stephen, appears simultaneously in two different systems of reference. In one he is the subject which manifests itself as "I"; in the other he is primarily the object, which is also capable of a kind of self-manifestation by means of the presentation of consciousness in narrated monologue. In the traditional novel the subject and object of presentation can become identical only when the third-person report of an authorial narrator is replaced by first-person direct discourse spoken by a third-person figure. In *Ulysses* the change from first-person to third-person reference—from subjective to objective presentation and back again—is accomplished gradually and with transitional stages. The above passage begins with a report. The reported action, however, is also perceived, to all appearances, by Stephen. Since the narrative situation in the preceding paragraph is clearly figural this report at the beginning of the passage will also be understood as figural presentation. Thus one cannot fix the boundary where this report turns into narrated monologue. The "lost Armada" is evidently an image evoked in Stephen by association with "wood sieved by the shipworm." But if "lost Armada," as a part of Stephen's consciousness, depends on "wood sieved by the shipworm," then this latter image must also be contained in his consciousness and thus also the parallel images "squeaking pebbles," "razorshells," and "damp crackling mast." The same also holds true for the next sentences. If "a sentinel" is a part of Stephen's consciousness, then what directly precedes this must also be supposed to be in Stephen's consciousness. The cataloguelike form of what follows "a sentinel" until the end of the paragraph is also characteristic. There are no verbs and pronouns to establish clearly tense and person. If this presentation of Stephen's consciousness is to be regarded as a form of narrated monologue, it should be noted that the third-person reference which would correspond to narrated monologue is not evoked in this cataloguelike part. It is thus conceivable that the first-person form of the interior monologue, which is used in the next paragraph, will cause the supposed narrated monologue to appear as interior monologue in retrospect.

The change in presentational forms and in references will not disturb the reader who has freed himself from the unity of narrative situation. In this way it becomes possible for the author to communicate the consciousness of his hero by three different paths of presentation, with three different degrees of stylization. The expressive potential of each individual mode of stylization is not difficult to infer from the initial discussion of the three kinds of presentation of consciousness. In *Ulysses* the thought report and narrated monologue represent primarily reflections of external events which could also be perceived by a person present on the scene. The interior monologue, on the other hand, generally presents the thoughts and feelings which arise from such perceptions in the figure's consciousness. In the former case one can thus still conceive of an objective narrator who participates in the knowledge of the facts; in the latter case, however, the completely subjective world of the figure leads to the more immediate form of rendering consciousness—the interior monologue. As yet no author has methodically extended the new paths indicated by Joyce's *Ulysses* for the presentation of consciousness in the novel.

VII

A TYPOLOGY OF THE NOVEL

IN HIS "Noten und Abhandlungen zu besserem Verständnis des west-östlichen Divans" Goethe distinguishes among three poetic modes or "Dichtweisen"—the clearly narrating, the enthusiastically excited, and the personally active modes; or epic, lyric, and drama. In the same section, "Naturformen der Dichtung," he goes on to say:

> These elements can be intertwined so marvelously, the poetic forms are infinitely manifold; and thus it is so difficult to find an order according to which one could arrange them one next to or after the other. But one will find some help if one places the three main elements across from each other in a circle and then seeks models in which each element exists alone. Then one should collect examples which tend in one direction or in the other, until the union of all three finally appears and thus the whole circle is closed in itself.[1]

Goethe's suggestion of a circular arrangement of the genres and of their intermediary forms was taken up by Julius Petersen. Several objections can be made to Petersen's genre ring, from which this study will single out only the epic sector with the novel forms contained there. The kinds of novels which Petersen places as intermediary forms between epic and lyric on the one side and between epic and drama on the other side seem to have been chosen rather arbitrarily. It is difficult, for example, to describe clearly the theoretical characteristic of his "lyrical novel," under which Petersen places a novel such as *Werther*. Petersen's genre circle, however, does not even justify the claims made for it by the author himself. Thus Petersen maintains: "The movement from lyric through the epic to the drama signifies a gradual withdrawal of the poet's person."[2] This is no doubt valid for the three genres if one views them in this sequence, but not for the intermediary forms indicated by Petersen. One may assume that the authorial novel, as the most traditional form of the novel, can be sought in Petersen's circle at or close to the location of the epic. But this already interrupts the line from lyric through epic to the drama—the line supposedly characterized by the gradual withdrawal of the author. At least in this respect one must conclude that Petersen has failed in attempting a continuous arrangement of the genres and their intermediary forms.

Goethe's suggestion of a circular arrangement of poetic forms which reveals the continuous transitions between the individual forms can also be realized in an entirely different manner. First it should be made clear that this is not an attempt to discover a genre circle along which one can enter all genres with their intermediary forms. Such a genre circle can only reveal the transitions between the possible poetic attitudes of expression; the "fundamental possibilities of human existence";[3] the lyrical, the epical, and the dramatical. It may be possible to show how the forms of poetry (in the larger sense) create a closed system by producing all conceivable forms through continuous variation of a single form. A typological circle which undertakes this task, however, can only be postulated for each individual genre. The results of the present study make it possible for the time being to prove this proposition with the forms of the novel.

Whenever the multiplicity of actual novels necessitates a classification, one encounters group divisions whose real *causa partitionis* lies in the realm of material and content. It is a common practice, for example, to distinguish among the travel novel, the sea novel, the adventure novel, the detective novel, the family novel, the generation novel, the developmental novel, and so forth. Such groups formed according to content, however, frequently also reveal important differences in structure and in the artistic organization of the content. The unilinear episodic sequence of the travel or adventure novel is clearly distinguished from the usual multilinear, broadly woven fabric of the family or generation novel. In the latter the predominant downward tendency of the action differs in a striking manner from the upward tendency of action in the developmental novel.

Wilhelm Dibelius purposely took such correspondences between content and structure as the starting point for a typology of the novel. His two main types, the adventure novel (Defoe, Fielding) and the novel of personality (Goldsmith, Richardson) are contrasted both according to the kind of plot motifs and characters (content!) and according to the "basic plan," "presentation," and "development of the action" (structure!).[4] At the end of his book on the narrative Robert Petsch postulates three types—saga, developmental novel, and the novel of events ("the pure novel")—which lack, to be sure, any unified basis of comparison. This is also the reason for the obvious incongruity in the size and definiteness of the individual types. Petsch also approaches his task by examining types of "epic process" as well as aspects of content.[5] There are numerous examples of similar attempts to establish typologies. The value of such typological undertakings for a genre theory of the novel is relatively small, though it cannot be denied that in individual cases a novel type established in this way can discover or reveal essential aspects of a novel. The reason for the relatively small theoretical significance of such typologies lies in the fact that they are so definite as to material and content. Such definiteness makes these categories capable of multiplication and proliferation *ad infinitum*. Where these typologies claim to establish types of structure or narrative process, however, their definition is usually quite circumstantial, since the types are derived from very complex theoretical relationships, rather than from the obvious facts of the narrative situation. In view of this general state of novel theory one must concur with Horst Oppel's observation that we are still a long way from a workable "typological pattern of organization for narrative forms."[6]

Edwin Muir's typological approach in *The Structure of the Novel* attempts to improve the state of novel theory. His three novel types—character novel, dramatic novel, and chronicle—correspond to the three perceptional categories of space, time, and causality. This is doubtless a step forward, beyond the narrowness of definitions based on content. Muir's typology of the novel was criticized in the introduction to this study.

A similar approach can be found in Wolfgang Kayser's differentiation between the novel of events, the novel of figures, and the novel of space in *Das sprachliche Kunstwerk*.[7] In his recent article, "Die Anfänge des modernen Romans im 18. Jahrhundert und seine heutige Krise," Kayser defines these types more precisely. It is evident that the novels of action, space, and figures, as he calls them, are meant as structural types. "The individual novel attains unity by taking either an action, or space (i.e. a multiplicity of places), or a figure as its basic structural level."[8] Yet since action, space, and figures are basic requisites of any event presented in a novel, it will be difficult in many works to discover whether action or space or figure is to be regarded as the structurally determining level. Nevertheless, these types represent a significant step forward in novel theory beyond the mere formation of groups according to content. They also cast light on aspects of novel structure which in general receive too little attention. Their theoretical value, however, will only prove useful in conjunction with the concrete facts of the narrative mode.

The clearest distinguishing characteristics of particular kinds of novels have received strikingly little attention in all these approaches. The concepts of the first-person novel, the third-person novel, the epistolary novel, and so forth, are in general circulation only as crude categories of rubrication. These concepts deserved to play this minor role as long as the distinctions they could provide remained of such highly superficial quality that little use could be made of them in a theory of the novel. These concepts have two advantages, however, which distinguish them from the other numerous, often very subtle differentiations of novel types. First, the concepts of the third-person novel and the first-person novel employ an aesthetic relationship as a principle of differentiation; these concepts are thus necessarily relevant to any theory of the novel. Second, the third-person novel and the first-person novel, as well as, for example, the epistolary novel, are categories which permit unambiguous classification of the individual novel without requiring a detailed discussion and definition of concepts.

A typological approach which attempts to take advantage of these concepts is faced with a twofold task. This approach must establish a relationship between these concepts and the novel's system of inner laws as manifested in interpretable form in the structure of the work; in doing so it must bring to light the specific theoretical significance of these concepts. Such a relationship, the narrative situation, is described in the introduction to this study and in the subsequent interpretations of individual works. In respect to the narrative situations which can predominate in a novel three novel types were distinguished: the authorial novel, the first-person novel, and the figural novel. The authorial novel and the figural novel are third-person forms. For the first-person novel, in turn, two possible forms were distinguished according to whether the narrative act is designated in the presentation or whether only the experiencing self penetrates into the reader's imagination. Other forms were shown to be variations of one of these three basic types, for example the epistolary novel as a special use of the narrative situation of the first-person novel with narrative act designated.

On the basis of narrative situation the structural characteristics of each novel type were determined. The structure of meaning of the authorial novel proved to be determined fundamentally by the relationship of tension between the narrator and the fictional world. This tension also provides an explanation for the authorial medium's guises; by means of these guises the authorial form of mediation is suited to the reader's illusion expectancy.

The nature of the relationships of the authorial medium to fictional reality also revealed the possibilities available to the authorial medium for transformation into a figural medium or into a first-person narrator. Two pathways were seen which ultimately point in opposite directions. While retaining the third-person reference the authorial medium can make less and less use of his privilege of Olympian superiority and independence in space and time, simultaneously supressing more and more its personal presence as narrator. In this way the impression arises that the fictional world is no longer mediated to the reader by the author and narrator, but rather by one or more figures of the fictional world. The author withdraws behind his characters. The reader no longer faces a narrator *in persona*; as in a play the reader seems to find himself before a scene, or he sees the fictional world mirrored in the consciousness of a fictional figure. The advantages of the figural narrative situation almost all lie in this circumstance of apparent immediacy which arises from the absence of a narrative distance perceivable to the reader. The processes of consciousness can be presented without interference and apparently without distortion by any kind of authorial manipulation. The reader himself senses an appeal to his power of judgment, since interpretation and commentary on the part of the author never become noticeable. The figural narrative situation, moreover, fixes the reader's center of orientation in the fictional scene; in this way the impression of "narrating" is largely suspended, while the impression of direct scenic presentation of the narrated material is strengthened.

If the authorial medium moves away from the authorial narrative situation in the opposite direction, however, then the third-person reference turns into a first-person reference. This first-person reference was already concealed in the authorial first-person reference; the author merely avoided referring to his own person in this way, since his person belongs to a completely different realm of existence from the characters in the novel. When the narrator steps over into the fictional world, or—from another standpoint—when the narrative process is incorporated into the fictional world, the narrating self enters into a quite unique relationship to his own past, to the experiencing self. Here the tension between the narrating self and experiencing self becomes structurally determinative under the condition that the narrative act receives corresponding presentation. The characteristic expressive potential of this narrative situation lies in the double refraction of the action—both in the perspective of the experiencing self and in the retrospection of the narrating self which now shows itself as more experienced, mature, and refined. The more the horizon of the fictional world closes in on the experiencing self, the more pale and formless the narrating self becomes, until finally it is fully invisible to the reader. But here the first-person novel reverts to the narrative situation of the figural novel, that is, a narrative situation characterized by the withdrawal of the narrative process behind the fictional scene or behind the direct mirroring of the contents of a figure's consciousness. Where, finally, the mere change of the pronoun from the first to the third person will turn the first-person novel into a figural novel—at this point the sector of the first-person novel borders on the sector of the figural novel.

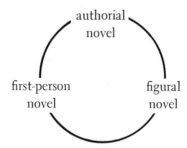

The possibility of continuously varying each novel type without interruption into each of the other two types proves that these three types do not lie in complete separation alongside one another in the realm of the genre. They represent, rather, the typical forms of the endlessly variable narrative situation of the novel. Their positions in relation to one another and the directions in which variation is conceivable can best be visualized in a circular pattern.

This typological circle contains the three main types of novel spaced at equal intervals; their relationship is similar to that which Goethe wanted to clarify by arranging the "poetic modes" in a genre circle. Between the poles of the authorial novel, the first-person novel, and the figural novel all evolving forms of the novel can be pinpointed in such a way that the structurally determinative feature of their narrative situation can be defined by their respective position on the typological circle, that is, by the distance from the two neighboring poles. In an authorial novel the typical narrative situation can be modified by the emergence of a personal link between the authorial medium and the fictional world. The author, for example, may cite a figure of the novel as his immediate informant. As soon as this modification takes place the location of this novel on the typological circle can be set still in the immediate proximity of the authorial pole, but displaced in the direction of the first-person novel. This displacement reflects the fact that the first-person pole designates a narrative situation in which the narrator stands completely within the realm of the fictional world. If one moves from the first-person pole in the direction of the authorial novel, on the other hand, one can pinpoint those first-person novels in which the actual narrative act is explicitly designated, since at the authorial pole the narrative act is most clearly pronounced. The more detailed the presentation of the narrating self, the closer such a first-person novel will move toward the pole of the authorial novel. On the other side of the first-person pole, in the direction of the figural novel, reference to the narrative act disappears into the background. The extreme form would be a first-person novel consisting solely of one interior monologue. The point of transition from interior monologue to narrated monologue—these two techniques differ here only by their use of the first or third-person reference—indicates the boundary between the first-person novel and the figural novel. The typological ring can then be closed between the figural and authorial poles if one adds the continuous series of those novel forms in which the author gradually emerges again *in persona*. Ultimately this leads the narrative situation of the figural novel back to that of the authorial novel.

If one were to determine the locations on this typological circle of all important novels of one or more literatures, a very revealing distribution would result. By far the greatest number of novels would crowd densely around the three poles; if one were to proceed historically the region of the figural novel would remain at first less populated, only to be filled later, however, by works written since the end of the last century. The number of works which would be pinpointed at a large distance from the poles would remain relatively small. From this observation one can conclude that not all possible narrative situations enjoy equal popularity among authors; certain narrative situations are obviously preferred. These preferred narrative situations, interestingly enough, stand close to the paradigmatic evolutions of the three novel types. The reason for such a tendency toward just a few fixed narrative forms can be found in the high potentiality and simultaneous simplicity of these typical forms. In the course of interpreting the individual works one could readily note one reason for the great formal potential of the paradigmatic forms of the novel. The reason lies in the simplicity of the narrative situation which corresponds to each of these types; a certain amount of modification is permissible in the employment of these narrative situations without detriment to the reader's illusion. Although in nonparadigmatic cases it is possible to create formally successful works which even surpass works employing the typical forms, such successes will almost always necessitate a corresponding increase in the complexity of the narrative situation.

The triad of types established in the present study is corroborated by the obvious correspondences between the narrative situations of these types and their respective forms for rendering consciousness. In the previous chapter three possibilities were defined for rendering consciousness—thought report, interior monologue, and the rendering of consciousness in narrated monologue. They correspond in this order to the narrative situations of the authorial novel, the first-person novel, and the figural novel.

The establishment of these three main types of novel is substantiated even more strikingly by the peculiar correspondence of the types to Emil Staiger's "basic modes of poetry"—the lyrical, the epical, and the dramatical modes. Without falling prey to the mysticism of the number three or to that of geometric forms, it is most convenient to illustrate this correspondence with a diagram. One can juxtapose, as Goethe did for the "Naturformen der Poesie," the three "basic modes"—lyrical, epical, and dramatical—in such a way that they form a circle or equilateral triangle. Then the typological circle of the novel may be drawn in the neighborhood of the epical mode with the au-

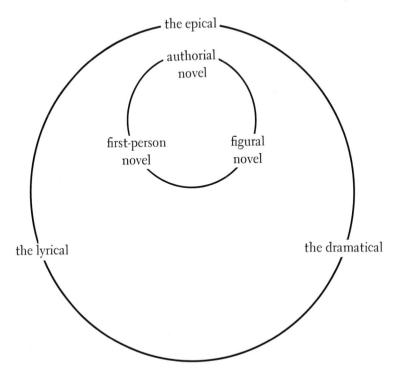

thorial pole opposite the place of the epical—the analogy between the authorial novel and the epical mode is the most obvious. If this is done a further correspondence immediately becomes visible between the first-person novel and the lyrical mode on the one hand, and the figural novel and the dramatical mode on the other.

It is not the purpose of this schema to demonstrate in detail the analogies between the "basic modes," lyrical, epical, dramatical, and the three novel types. This should not prove difficult for the authorial novel and the epical, or for the figural novel and the dramatic. The problem is somewhat different for the relationship between the first-person novel and the lyrical mode. Moreover, in such a specialized application Emil Staiger's definition of the "basic modes" can only serve to clarify partial aspects of the relationship, since this definition was undertaken without sufficient consideration of the novel. Only a redefinition of the "basic modes" which includes the structural peculiarities of the novel and its forms could perhaps advance beyond the recognition of the already obvious parallels between the three novel types and the three "basic modes."

For literary theory the decisive conclusion which can be drawn from this schema is of a different nature. It has more than once become clear from the individual interpretations that a novel with a given narrative situation will also contain the narrative situations of the other two types to a certain degree. Approximations, partial assumption of the conventions characteristic of the other two narrative situations, for a time even complete transition to a narrative situation of the other type are all possible. It can therefore be said that the individual narrative work establishes one dominant narrative situation, but that the remaining two possibilities of presentation are kept concealed under the external guise of the narrative process. Thus it is possible to resort to them in special instances. Only this circumstance makes it possible to pinpoint all forms of the novel on a typological circle which shows the continuity of variation from form to form and ultimately from type to type.

This observation only reveals its full significance when seen in relationship to the "basic modes," as shown in the diagram. Once a given narrative work has been assigned on the basis of its narrative situation to a definite location on the typological circle, the work will stand in a corresponding relationship to all the other poles on the circle. The pole closest to each narrative work, in turn, stands in a corresponding relationship to one of the three "basic poetic modes." The genres or "Naturformen der Poesie" are really abstractions based on concrete literary realizations of the three "basic modes" or kinds of human attitude— the epical, the lyrical, and the dramatical. The relationships between the genres, should one accept Goethe's testimony, are similar to those which prevail between the three basic types of novel, since both the genres and the types can be shown to vary in a continuous progression from one to the next.

Further deductions would lead one dangerously close to purely theoretical speculation. Perhaps what has already been said will serve to call the attention of genre theory and of all literary theory to the relationship which exists between an individual work and the incontrovertible categories of poetics. This relationship is a promising one, for here, too, poetic theory need only systematize what has long been known in individual interpretations, if only intuitively: in every creative work of literature all other formal possibilities, structures, and genres collaborate in a peculiar, furtive way. Thus an attempt to find types, to outline genres, will inevitably do some violence to the indescribable totality in which each individual element participates. Such an approach, no matter how imposing the evidence which supports it, always calls for skepticism—skepticism which can only give way when the approach reveals an inexhaustible potential for interpretation in the individual literary work.

BIBLIOGRAPHY

THE BIBLIOGRAPHY includes only those works to which explicit reference has been made.

Abbreviations:

DVLG—*Deutsche Vierteljahrsschrift für Literaturwissenschaft und Geistesgeschichte*
GRM— *Germanisch-Romanische Monatsschrift*
PMLA—*Publications of the Modern Language Association of America*

Ament, William S. "Bowdler and the Whale," *American Literature,* IV (1932), 39 ff.
Auerbach, Erich. *Mimesis: Dargestellte Wirklichkeit in der abendländischen Literatur.* Bern, 1946.
Austen, Jane. *Northanger Abbey.* London, 1913.
————. *Pride and Prejudice.* London, 1911.
Beach, Joseph Warren. *The Twentieth Century Novel: Studies in Technique.* New York, 1932.
Bennett, Arnold. *The Author's Craft.* New York, 1914.
Börsenverein deutscher Verleger- und Buchhändler-Verbände E. V., ed. *Buch und Buchhandel in Zahlen.* Frankfurt am Main, 1953.
Booth, Wayne C. "The Self-conscious Narrator in Comic Fiction Before *Tristram Shandy,*" PMLA, LXVII (1952), 163 ff.
Bowling, Lawrence E. "What is the Stream of Consciousness Technique?" PMLA, LXV (1950), 333 ff.

Brentano, Clemens. *Godwi oder das steinerne Bild der Mutter.* Bremen, 1802.

Brontë, Emily. *Wuthering Heights.* London, 1907.

Bunyan, John. *The Pilgrim's Progress.* Oxford, 1879.

Camus, Albert. *The Rebel: An Essay on Man in Revolt.* New York, 1967.

Canby, Henry Seidel. *Turn West, Turn East: Mark Twain and Henry James.* Boston, 1951.

Capote, Truman. *The Grass Harp.* New York, 1953.

Cary, Joyce. *Mister Johnson.* London, 1947.

Cervantes, Saavedra Miguel de. *Don Quixote de la Mancha.* Berlin, 1928.

Conrad, Joseph. *The Nigger of the Narcissus.* London, 1946.

Curtius, Ernst Robert. *James Joyce und sein "Ulysses."* Zurich, 1929.

Defoe, Daniel. *Moll Flanders.* London, 1948.

Dibelius, Wilhelm. *Englische Romankunst: Die Technik des englischen Romans im achtzehnten und zu Anfang des neunzehnten Jahrhunderts.* Berlin, 1910.

Dickens, Charles. *David Copperfield.* Leipzig, 1849.

Dujardin, Edouard. *Les Lauriers sont coupés.* Paris, 1924.

————. *Le Monologue intérieur.* Paris, 1931.

Dupee, F. W. *Henry James.* London, 1951.

Eliot, T. S. "Ulysses, Order, and Myth," in *James Joyce: Two Decades of Criticism,* ed. Seon Givens. New York, 1948.

Farrell, James T. *My Days of Anger.* New York, 1943.

Faulkner, William. *Light in August.* New York, 1932.

————. *The Sound and the Fury.* New York, 1946.

————. *Absalom, Absalom!* New York, 1951.

Fehr, Bernhard. "James Joyces *Ulysses,*" *Englische Studien,* LX (1925–26), 180 ff.

————. *Englische Prosa von 1880 bis zur Gegenwart.* Leipzig, 1927.

————. "Substitutionary Narration and Description," *Von Englands geistigen Beständen.* Frauenfeld, 1944.

Fielding, Henry. *Joseph Andrews.* London: George Routledge, n.d.

————. *The History of Tom Jones, A Foundling.* Edinburgh, 1767.

Forster, E. M. *Aspects of the Novel.* New York, 1927.

Friedemann, Käte. *Die Rolle des Erzählers in der Epik.* Leipzig, 1910.

Funke, Otto. " 'Erlebte Rede' bei Galsworthy," *Englische Studien,* LXIV (1929), 450 ff.

Gilbert, Stuart. *James Joyce's Ulysses.* New York, 1938.

Givens, Seon, ed. *James Joyce: Two Decades of Criticism.* New York, 1948.

Glauser, Lisa. *Die erlebte Rede im englischen Roman des 19. Jahrhunderts.* Bern, 1948.

Goethe, J. W. *West-östlicher Divan,* ed. Ernst Beutler. Leipzig, 1943.

Greene, Graham. "Introduction" to Henry James, *The Portrait of a Lady.* London, 1947.

Günther, Werner. *Die Probleme der Rededarstellung.* Marburg, 1928.

Hamburger, Käte. "Zum Strukturproblem der epischen und dramatischen Dichtung," *DVLG,* XXV (1951), 1 ff.

————. "Das epische Praeteritum," *DVLG,* XXVII (1953), 329 ff.

Hemingway, Ernest. "The Killers," in *The Essential Hemingway.* London, 1948.

Ingarden, Roman. *Das literarische Kunstwerk: Eine Untersuchung aus dem Grenzgebiet der Ontologie, Logik, und Literaturwissenschaft.* Halle/Saale, 1931.

James, Henry. *The Portrait of a Lady.* New York: The Modern Library, n. d.

————. *The Golden Bowl.* New York, 1923.

————. *The Wings of the Dove.* New York, 1937.

————. *The Ambassadors.* New York, 1948.

————. *The Art of the Novel: Critical Prefaces,* intr. Richard P. Blackmur. New York, 1950.

————. *The Notebooks,* ed. F. O. Matthiessen and Kenneth B. Murdock. New York, 1947.

————, and Walter Besant. *The Art of Fiction.* Boston: DeWolfe and Fiske, n.d.

James, William. *The Principles of Psychology.* London, 1890.

Jespersen, Otto. *A Modern English Grammar* I. Heidelberg, 1909.

Jones, Howard Mumford. *Guide to American Literature and Its Backgrounds Since 1890.* Cambridge, Mass., 1953.

Joyce, James. *A Portrait of the Artist as a Young Man.* London, 1926.

————. *Ulysses.* New York, 1934.

Jung, C. G. *Wirklichkeit der Seele.* Zurich, 1939.

Jungel, Renate. "Die Zeitstruktur in den Romanen E. M. Forsters." Unpublished dissertation, Graz, 1953.

Karpf, Fritz. "Die erlebte Rede im Englischen," *Anglia,* LVII (1933), 225 ff.

Kayser, Wolfgang. *Das sprachliche Kunstwerk: Eine Einführung in die Literaturwissenschaft.* Bern, 1948.

————. "Die Anfänge des modernen Romans im 18. Jahrhundert und seine heutige Krise," *DVLG*, XXVIII (1954), 417 ff.

Kettle, Arnold. *An Introduction to the English Novel.* London, I, 1951, II, 1953.

Koskimies, Rafael. *Theorie des Romans.* Helsinki, 1935.

Larbaud, Valéry. "James Joyce," *Nouvelle revue française,* (April, 1922), 385–409.

Lawrence, D. H. *The Rainbow.* Hamburg, 1934.

————. *Phoenix: The Posthumous Papers of D. H. Lawrence.* London, 1936.

————. *The Letters,* ed. A. Huxley, The Albatross Collected Edition, Leipzig, 1939.

————. *Women in Love.* London, 1948.

Leavis, F. R. *The Great Tradition.* London, 1948.

Levin, Harry. *James Joyce: A Critical Introduction.* Norfolk, Conn., 1941.

Lewis, Wyndham. *Time and Western Man.* London, 1927.

Leyda, Jay. *The Melville Log: A Documentary Life of Herman Melville 1819 to 1891.* New York, 1951.

Lubbock, Percy. *The Craft of Fiction.* New York, 1931.

Ludwig, Otto. "Formen der Erzählung" in *Gesammelte Schriften,* ed. A. Stern. vol. VI, Leipzig, 1891.

Mann, Thomas. *Der Zauberberg.* Stockholm, 1946.

Mansfield, Luther S., and Howard P. Vincent. "Explanatory Notes" in *Moby-Dick or, The Whale.* New York, 1952.

Matthiessen, F. O. *Henry James: The Major Phase.* London, 1946.

Melville, Herman. *Typee.* London: Everyman's Library, n.d.

————. *Omoo.* London, 1893.

————. *Moby-Dick or, The Whale,* ed. Luther S. Mansfield and Howard P. Vincent. New York, 1952.

Mendilow, A. A. *Time and the Novel.* London, 1952.

Merker, Paul and Wolfgang Stammler, eds. *Reallexikon der deutschen Literaturgeschichte,* vol. III. Berlin, 1928–29.

Muir, Edwin. *The Structure of the Novel.* London, 1928.

Müller, Günther. *Die Gestaltfrage in der Literaturwissenschaft.* Halle/Saale, 1944.

————. "Erzählzeit und erzählte Zeit," in *Festschrift für Paul Kluckhohn und Herman Schneider.* Tübingen, 1948.

————. "Über das Zeitgerüst des Erzählens," *DVLG,* XXIV (1950), 1 ff.

_____. "Die Aufbauformen des Romans," *Neophilologus*, XXVII (1953), 1 ff.

Nashe, Thomas. *The Unfortunate Traveller*. London, 1892.

O'Connor, William Van, ed. *Forms of Modern Fiction*. Minneapolis, 1948.

Oppel, Horst. *Die Kunst des Erzählens im englischen Roman des 19. Jahrhunderts*. Bielefeld, 1950.

Petersen, Julius. *Die Wissenschaft von der Dichtung*. Berlin, 1939.

Petsch, Robert. "Epische Grundformen." *GRM*, XVI (1928), 379–99.

_____. *Wesen und Formen der Erzählkunst*. Halle/Saale, 1934.

Rickwood, C. H. "A Note on Fiction" in *Forms of Modern Fiction*, ed. W. Van O'Connor. Minneapolis, 1948.

Schiller, Friedrich. "Über naive und sentimentalische Dichtung." Säkular-Ausgabe XII, 1904, 161 ff.

Schnitzler, Arthur. *Ausgewählte Erzählungen*. Frankfurt am Main, 1950.

Shipley, Joseph T. *Dictionary of World Literature*. New York, 1943.

Sihler, Helmut. "Die Zeitstruktur der Romane von John Dos Passos." Unpublished dissertation, Graz, 1953.

Smollett, Tobias. *Roderick Random*. Leipzig, 1845.

_____. *Peregrine Pickle*. Leipzig, 1870.

Sosnosky, Theodor von. "Die Unnatur der Ich-Erzählung," *Die Gegenwart*, 1902, pp. 309 ff. and pp. 325 ff.

Spielhagen, Friedrich. *Beiträge zur Theorie und Technik des Romans*. Leipzig, 1883.

_____. *Neue Beiträge zur Theorie und Technik der Epik und Dramatik*. Leipzig, 1898.

Spitzer, Leo. "Sprachmischung als Stilmittel und als Ausdruck der Klangphantasie," *GRM*, XI (1923), 193 ff.

Staiger, Emil. *Grundbegriffe der Poetik*. Zurich, 1946.

Stanzel, Franz. "Die Zeitgestaltung in William Faulkners *The Bear*," *Die Neueren Sprachen*, 1953, p. 114 ff.

_____. "Die Erzählsituation in Virginia Woolfs *Jacob's Room*, *Mrs. Dalloway*, und *To the Lighthouse*," *GRM*, N. F. IV (1954), 196 ff.

_____. "*Tom Jones* und *Tristram Shandy*: Ein Vergleich als Vorstudie zu einer Typologie des Romans," *English Miscellany*, V, (Rom, 1954), 107 ff.

Steinbeck, John. *Of Mice and Men*. New York, 1937.

_____. *The Pearl* and *Burning Bright*. London, 1954.

Sterne, Laurence. *Tristram Shandy*. London, 1900.

Stewart, George R. "The Two Moby-Dicks," *American Literature*, XXV (1954), 417 ff.

Strong, L. A. G. *The Sacred River: An Approach to James Joyce*. London, 1949.

Thackeray, W. M. *The History of Henry Esmond Written by Himself*. London, n.d.

Times Literary Supplement, The. London. July 23, 1954, Lead Article, p. 437.

Toynbee, Philip. *Tea with Mrs. Goodman*. London, 1947.

Trollope, Anthony. *Barchester Towers*. Leipzig, 1859.

Walzel, Oskar. *Das Wortkunstwerk*. Leipzig, 1926.

Warren, Robert Penn. *All the King's Men*. New York, 1951.

Wellek, René, and Austin Warren. *Theory of Literature*. New York, 1949.

Werfel, Franz. *Das Lied von Bernadette*. Vienna, 1948.

Woolf, Virginia. *The Common Reader* (First Series). London, 1925.

————. *Mrs. Dalloway*. Leipzig, 1929.

————. *The Captain's Death Bed*. London, 1950.

Wright, Andrew H. *Jane Austen's Novels: A Study in Structure*. London, 1953.

Zeller, Hildegard. *Die Ich-Erzählung im englischen Roman*. Breslau, 1933.

NOTES

INTRODUCTION

1. Howard Mumford Jones, *Guide to American Literature and Its Backgrounds Since 1890* (Cambridge, Mass., 1953), p. 47 and *Buch und Buchhandel in Zahlen* (Frankfurt am Main, 1953), p. 7.

2. Roman Ingarden, *Das literarische Kunstwerk* (Halle/Saale, 1931), p. 303.

3. *The Times Literary Supplement*, July 23, 1954, Lead Article, p. 437.

4. See the examples in Käte Friedemann, *Die Rolle des Erzählers in der Epik* (Leipzig, 1910), p. 28 ff.

5. Friedrich von Schiller, "Über naive und sentimentalische Dichtung," Säkular-Ausgabe, XII, 200, 216.

6. Emil Staiger, *Grundbegriffe der Poetik* (Zurich, 1946), p. 90 ff.

7. See Rafael Koskimies, *Theorie des Romans* (Helsinki, 1935), esp. p. 71 ff.

8. See Friedrich Spielhagen, *Beiträge zur Theorie und Technik des Romans* (Leipzig, 1883), esp. p. 220.

9. Robert Petsch, *Wesen und Formen der Erzählkunst* (Halle/Saale, 1934), p. 57.

10. Friedemann, p. 25.

11. Julius Petersen, *Die Wissenschaft von der Dichtung* (Berlin, 1939), p. 130.

12. Ingarden, p. 303.

13. Ibid., p. 225.

14. Ibid., p. 343.

15. Petsch, pp. 4–5.

16. Albert Camus, *The Rebel: An Essay on Man in Revolt.* (New York, 1967), p. 269

17. E. M. Forster, *Aspects of the Novel* (New York, 1927), p. 63.

18. Cf. F. O. Matthiessen, *Henry James: The Major Phase* (London, 1946), p. 183; F. W. Dupee, *Henry James* (London, 1951), p. 124; and Graham Greene, "Introduction" to *The Portrait of a Lady* (London, 1947), p. viii.

19. Henry Seidel Canby, *Turn West, Turn East: Mark Twain and Henry James* (Boston, 1951), p. 261.

20. Günther Müller, *Die Gestaltfrage in der Literaturwissenschaft,* (Halle/Saale, 1944), p. 28.

21. Arnold Kettle, *An Introduction to the English Novel* (London, 1951), I, 13.

22. Ibid., I, 15.

23. Forster, p. 128.

24. Ibid., p. 215.

25. Edwin Muir, *The Structure of the Novel* (London, 1928), esp. p. 113 f.

26. See Günther Müller, "Erzählzeit und erzählte Zeit" in *Festschrift für Paul Kluckhohn und Hermann Schneider* (Tübingen, 1948): and "Über das Zeitgerüst des Erzählens," DVLG, XXIV (1950), 1 ff.

27. See A. A. Mendilow, *Time and the Novel* (London, 1952).

28. Petsch, p. 96 ff.

29. Horst Oppel, *Die Kunst des Erzählens im englischen Roman des 19. Jahrhunderts* (Bielefeld, 1950).

30. Günther Müller, "Die Aufbauformen des Romans," *Neophilologus,* XXVII (1953), p. 8.

31. D. H. Lawrence, *Phoenix* (London, 1936), p. 308.

32. Cf. D. H. Lawrence, *The Letters of D. H. Lawrence* (Leipzig, 1939), I, 192, 225, 261, *passim*; II, 108.

33. Ibid., II, 292.

34. Ibid., I, 99.

I. The Narrative Situation and the Epic Preterite

1. Otto Ludwig, "Formen der Erzählung," *Gesammelte Schriften* (Leipzig, 1891), VI, 202 ff.

2. Cf. Friedrich Spielhagen, *Neue Beiträge zur Theorie und Technik der Epik und Dramatik* (Leipzig, 1898), p. 55 ff.

3. Emil Staiger, *Grundbegriffe der Poetik* (Zurich, 1946), p. 92 f.

4. See Rafael Koskimies, *Theorie des Romans* (Helsinki, 1935), p. 120; Wolfgang Kayser, "Die Anfänge des modernen Romans im 18. Jahrhundert und seine heutige Krise," *DVLG*, XXVIII (1954), esp. 429 ff.

5. Käte Friedemann, *Die Rolle des Erzählers in der Epik* (Leipzig, 1910), p. 3.

6. Robert Petsch, "Epische Grundformen," *GRM*, XVI (1928), 381.

7. Ludwig, VI, 204–05.

8. Percy Lubbock, *The Craft of Fiction* (New York, 1931), p. 156 ff.

9. Robert Petsch, *Wesen und Formen der Erzählkunst* (Halle/Saale, 1934), p. 331.

10. See Oskar Walzel, *Das Wortkunstwerk* (Leipzig, 1926), p. 201 ff.

11. The concept of the center of orientation used here is taken from Roman Ingarden, *Das literarische Kunstwerk* (Halle/Saale, 1931), pp. 232–33. Since Ingarden still regards the authorial narrative act as a part of fictional reality, the center of orientation is for him always within the realm of fictional reality. In this study, however, the authorial narrative act will be regarded as outside fictional reality.

12. Käte Hamburger, "Das epische Praeteritum," *DVLG*, XXVII (1953), 332.

13. Petsch, *Wesen und Formen*, pp. 93–94.

14. Wolfgang Kayser, *Das sprachliche Kunstwerk* (Bern, 1948), p. 351.

15. Julius Petersen, *Die Wissenschaft von der Dichtung* (Berlin, 1939), pp. 123 ff. and 155.

16. Staiger, p. 93.

17. Ibid., p. 236.

18. Ingarden, p. 232 f.

19. Käte Hamburger, "Zum Strukturproblem der epischen und dramatischen Dichtung," *DVLG*, XXV (1951), 4.

20. Hamburger, "Das epische Praeteritum," 354 ff.

21. Ibid., 333.

II. The Authorial Novel: *Tom Jones*

1. Henry James and Walter Besant, *The Art of Fiction* (Boston, n.d.), p. 55.

2. Ibid., p. 54.

3. Henry James, *The Art of the Novel: Critical Prefaces* (New York, 1950), p. 222.

4. Arnold Bennett, *The Author's Craft* (New York, 1914), p. 60.

5. Henry Fielding, *Tom Jones*, Book IX, Chapter VII.

6. Cf. also Franz Stanzel, *"Tom Jones* und *Tristram Shandy,"* *English Miscellany*, V (1954), esp. 109 ff.

7. Cf. Käte Friedemann, *Die Rolle des Erzählers in der Epik* (Leipzig, 1910), p. 88 ff., where further examples of this play with the reader's illusion can be found.

8. On the concept of narrative distance see also Stanzel, 128 ff.

9. Renate Jungel, "Die Zeitstruktur in den Romanen E. M. Forsters" (Graz, 1953), p. 69, n. 1.

10. Cf. Percy Lubbock, *The Craft of Fiction* (New York, 1931), p. 72 f.

11. On the concept of compression or *Raffung* see Horst Oppel, *Die Kunst des Erzählens im englischen Roman des 19. Jahrhunderts* (Bielefeld, 1950). Using the previous studies of Günther Müller, Oppel distinguishes three kinds of compression. Renate Jungel's study of the novels of E. M. Forster develops the concepts of intermittent, punctual, and durative compression (pp. 26–27). Helmut Sihler introduces the concept of the iterative report in his study of the novels of John Dos Passos; cf. "Die Zeitstruktur der Romane von John Dos Passos" (Graz, 1953), p. 60.

12. See Oppel, esp. pp. 47 and 55.

13. Wilhelm Dibelius, *Englische Romankunst* (Berlin, 1910), I, 159 ff.

14. On the time structure of *Tom Jones* see Stanzel, p. 133 ff.

15. Cf. Otto Jespersen, *A Modern English Grammar* (Heidelberg, 1909), I, 7, 33; and Fritz Karpf, "Die erlebte Rede im Englischen," *Anglia*, LVII (1933), 234.

16. Cf. F. R. Leavis on *Tom Jones:* "There can't be subtlety of organization without richer matter to organize, and subtler interests, than Fielding has to offer." *The Great Tradition* (London, 1948), p. 4.

17. Friedemann, p. 26.

18. Andrew H. Wright, *Jane Austen's Novels* (London, 1953), p. 71.

19. Lubbock, p. 156 ff.

20. E. M. Forster, *Aspects of the Novel* (New York, 1927), p. 119.

21. See Franz Stanzel, "Die Erzählsituation in Virginia Woolfs

Jacob's Room, Mrs. Dalloway, und *To the Lighthouse,*" GRM, N.F. IV (1954), esp. 202 ff.

22. See Leo Spitzer, "Sprachmischung als Stilmittel und als Ausdruck der Klangphantasie," GRM, XI (1923), 193 ff.

III. THE FIRST-PERSON NOVEL

1. Cf. William M. Thackeray, *Henry Esmond* (London, n.d.), pp. 119, 123, 175, 191, 317.

2. See Franz Stanzel, *"Tom Jones* und *Tristram Shandy,"* *English Miscellany* V (1954), 141 ff.

3. All quotations are taken from the edition by Luther S. Mansfield and Howard P. Vincent (New York, 1952). The "Explanatory Notes" provided by the two editors will be referred to as "Notes."

4. George R. Stewart, "The Two Moby-Dicks," *American Literature,* XXV (1954), 417 ff.

5. Cf. Luther S. Mansfield and Howard P. Vincent, "Notes," p. 831.

6. Cf. Jay Leyda, *The Melville Log* (New York, 1951), I, 417 and 427.

7. Cf. "Notes," p. 831.

8. Cf. "Notes," p. 783.

9. Cf. Leyda, I, 401.

10. Cf. William S. Ament, "Bowdler and the Whale," *American Literature,* IV (1932), 39 ff.

11. Stewart, p. 435.

12. Theodor von Sosnosky, "Die Unnatur der Ich-Erzählung," *Die Gegenwart,* 1902, pp. 309 ff. and pp. 325 ff.

13. See Hildegard Zeller, *Die Ich-Erzählung im englischen Roman* (Breslau, 1933), esp. p. 17 ff.

14. Cf. Käte Hamburger, "Das epische Praeteritum," DVLG, XXVII (1953), 354 ff.

15. Ibid., 357.

IV. THE FIGURAL NOVEL

1. Wolfgang Kayser, "Die Anfänge des modernen Romans im 18. Jahrhundert und seine heutige Krise," DVLG, XXVIII (1954), 417 ff.

2. Ibid., 445.

3. See Virginia Woolf, *The Common Reader*, First Series (London, 1925), p. 189 ff.

4. John Steinbeck, *Burning Bright* (London, 1954), p. 85.

5. The genesis of *The Ambassadors* preceeds that of *The Wings of the Dove*. The actual writing of *The Ambassadors* had apparently already begun in the summer of 1900.

6. F. O. Matthiessen and Kenneth B. Murdock, ed., *The Notebooks of Henry James* (New York, 1947). The scenario to *The Ambassadors* can be found at the end (pp. 372–415) of this edition.

7. Henry James, *The Art of the Novel Critical Prefaces* (New York, 1950), pp. 320–21.

8. Ibid., p. 321.

9. *Loc. cit.*

10. *Loc. cit.*

11. Quotations are taken from *The Ambassadors* (New York, 1948).

12. James, *Prefaces*, p. 322.

13. Ibid., p. 321.

14. Ibid., p. 323.

15. Philip Toynbee, *Tea with Mrs. Goodman* (London, 1947).

16. Roman Ingarden, *Das literarische Kunstwerk* (Halle/Saale, 1931), p. 241.

17. Robert Petsch, *Wesen und Formen der Erzählkunst* (Halle/Saale, 1934), p. 98.

18. Franz Stanzel, "Die Zeitgestaltung in William Faulkners *The Bear*," *Die Neueren Sprachen*, 1953, p. 120.

19. Ingarden, p. 236.

20. *Notebooks*, p. 374.

21. Ibid., pp. 377 and 388.

V. Ulysses

1. Quotations are taken from the Modern Library edition (New York, 1946). This edition contains a number of typographical errors, but it is the most readily available.

2. C. H. Rickwood, "A Note on Fiction" in *Forms of Modern Fiction* (Minneapolis, 1948), p. 305.

3. Seon Givens, ed., *James Joyce: Two Decades of Criticism* (New York, 1948), p. 201; cited below as *Two Decades*.

4. Stuart Gilbert, *James Joyce's Ulysses* (New York, 1938), p. 174.

5. Ernst Robert Curtius, *James Joyce und sein "Ulysses"* (Zurich, 1929), p. 52.

6. Gilbert, p. 239.

7. L. A. G. Strong, *The Sacred River: An Approach to James Joyce* (London, 1949), p. 33.

8. Harry Levin, *James Joyce: A Critical Introduction* (Norfolk, Conn., 1941).

9. *Two Decades*, p. 211.

10. Gilbert, p. 236.

11. Curtius, p. 55.

12. Loc. cit.

13. *Reallexikon der deutschen Literaturgeschichte* (Berlin, 1928–29), III, 337–38.

14. Cf. Harry Levin, p. 71: "The Homeric overtones do contribute their note of universality, their range of tradition, to what might well be a trivial and colorless tale. But in so doing, they convert a realistic novel into a mock-epic."

15. Stanzel, *"Tom Jones* und *Tristram Shandy," English Miscellany*, V (1954), 113–14.

16. Erich Auerbach, *Mimesis: Dargestellte Wirklichkeit in der abendländischen Literatur* (Bern, 1946), p. 413.

17. Gilbert, p. 291.

18. Philip Toynbee sees in this chapter the language and style of a "provincial gossip column." Cf. *Two Decades*, p. 280.

19. pp. 623, 633, 644.

20. *Two Decades*, p. 281.

21. Bernhard Fehr, "James Joyces *Ulysses*," *Englische Studien*, LX (1925–1926), 202.

22. Arnold Kettle holds the opposite opinion. Cf. *An Introduction to the English Novel* (London, 1953), II, 136–37.

23. C. G. Jung, *Wirklichkeit der Seele* (Zurich, 1939).

24. Ibid., p. 167.

VI. Excursus: The Rendering of Consciousness

1. Wyndham Lewis, *Time and Western Man* (London, 1927), esp. p. 122.

2. See Edouard Dujardin, *Le Monologue intérieur* (Paris, 1931).

3. Valéry Larbaud, "James Joyce," *Nouvelle revue française*, April 1922, pp. 335–409.

4. Cf. René Wellek and Austin Warren, *Theory of Literature* (New York, 1949), p. 233; and Joseph T. Shipley, *Dictionary of World Literature* (New York, 1943), p. 384.

5. Lawrence E. Bowling, "What is the Stream of Consciousness Technique?" *PMLA*, LXV (1950), esp. 345.

6. Bernhard Fehr, "Substitutionary Narration and Description" in *Von Englands geistigen Beständen* (Frauenfeld, 1944), p. 264 ff.

7. Percy Lubbock, *The Craft of Fiction* (New York, 1931), p. 162.

8. Bernhard Fehr, *Englische Prosa von 1880 bis zur Gegenwart* (Leipzig, 1927), p. 34.

9. Werner Günther, *Die Probleme der Rededarstellung* (Marburg, 1928), pp. 85–86.

10. In addition to the numerous general works on narrated monologue see especially the following studies of narrated monologue in English: Otto Funke, " 'Erlebte Rede' bei Galsworthy," *Englische Studien*, LXIV (1929), 450 ff.; Fritz Karpf, "Die erlebte Rede im Englischen," *Anglia*, LVII (1933), 225 ff.; and Bernhard Fehr, "Substitutionary Narration and Description," p. 264.

11. Käte Hamburger, "Das epische Praeteritum," *DVLG*, XXVII (1953), 345.

12. Lisa Glauser, *Die erlebte Rede im englischen Roman des 19. Jahrhunderts* (Bern, 1948).

VII. A TYPOLOGY OF THE NOVEL

1. Johann Wolfgang von Goethe, *West-östlicher Divan* (Leipzig, 1943), p. 221.

2. Julius Petersen, *Die Wissenschaft von der Dichtung* (Berlin, 1939), p. 123 ff.

3. Emil Staiger, *Grundbegriffe der Poetik* (Zurich, 1946), p. 226.

4. Wilhelm Dibelius, *Englische Romankunst* (Berlin, 1910), esp. I, 26–27.

5. Robert Petsch, *Wesen und Formen der Erzählkunst* (Halle/Saale, 1934), p. 281 ff.

6. Horst Oppel, *Die Kunst des Erzählens im englischen Roman des 19. Jahrhunderts* (Bielefeld, 1950), p. 25.

7. Wolfgang Kayser, *Das sprachliche Kunstwerk* (Bern, 1948), p. 362 ff.

8. Wolfgang Kayser, "Die Anfänge des modernen Romans im 18. Jahrhundert und seine heutige Krise," *DVLG*, XXVIII (1954), 438.

I N D E X

185